T0148576

ELEMENTARY MARINE NAVIGATION

by

S. A. WALLING
Senior Master, R.N. (Ret.)

and

J. C. HILL, B.A. (CANTAB.)
Education Department, Cambridge University Press

CAMBRIDGE
AT THE UNIVERSITY PRESS
1944

CONTENTS

MAP OF BISHOP ROCK AND BERRY HEAD
available for download from www.cambridge.org/9781107419414

CAMBRIDGE
UNIVERSITY PRESS

University Printing House, Cambridge CB2 8BS, United Kingdom

Published in the United States of America by Cambridge University Press, New York

Cambridge University Press is part of the University of Cambridge.

It furthers the University's mission by disseminating knowledge in the pursuit of
education, learning and research at the highest international levels of excellence.

www.cambridge.org
Information on this title: www.cambridge.org/9781107419414

© Cambridge University Press 1944

This publication is in copyright. Subject to statutory exception
and to the provisions of relevant collective licensing agreements,
no reproduction of any part may take place without the written
permission of Cambridge University Press.

First published 1944
First paperback edition 2014

A catalogue record for this publication is available from the British Library

ISBN 978-1-107-41941-4 Paperback

Cambridge University Press has no responsibility for the persistence or accuracy of
URLs for external or third-party internet websites referred to in this publication,
and does not guarantee that any content on such websites is, or will remain, accurate
or appropriate.

FOREWORD

by

INSTRUCTOR REAR-ADMIRAL A. E. HALL, C.B., C.B.E.
Director of Education, Admiralty

When we are young, it is always a most thrilling event for us to find out how any of the facts we learn at school are made use of in real life. Most of our school learning is as essential to us—if we are to play a useful part in the world—as is the alphabet which enables us to read and write. I well remember the excitement of learning about the working of the magnetic compass, the electric bell and the filament lamp in my electricity classes, while even the common pump and the crowbar gave a touch of reality to the study of mechanics. Such a sense of purpose was a tremendous aid to study.

Of special interest therefore to the youth of a seafaring country is the story of the application of some simple facts of mathematics to the practice of navigation. You will begin to learn how to find your way about the great oceans, which have been of such great importance in our island history. This book introduces you, in an easy and interesting way, to the elements of marine navigation and shows you how some simple rules of geometry are used by sailors. It should be a valuable aid to a young man wishing to probe the mysteries of navigation. It will thus serve the very useful purpose of preparing members of the Sea Cadet Corps against the time when they will join the Navy and will learn about the subject from other more advanced books.

The practical examples in this book will be of great value to the youthful student. As in everything that is worth doing, it is practice that produces accuracy and quickness of work. You should therefore enjoy the practical exercises included in this book, which, though dealing only with the simpler applications, illustrate the actual methods used by the Royal Navy and the Merchant Navy.

I have very great pleasure in introducing a book which should arouse in the youth of this country an interest in navigation and a love of the sea, and which may provide an incentive to travel and adventure.

a Ettall

1 *September* 1943

PREFACE

The authors offer this little book as a logical sequel to *Nautical Mathematics* so that the simple geometrical principles which in most cases will already have been studied may be applied to some of their various uses at sea.

The study of elementary marine navigation calls for little beyond the accurate use of ordinary geometrical instruments and the construction of simple scale drawings. It is the application and method that affords the exercise and the interest. Proficiency can be attained only by constant practice in the working of the many different and typical problems of elementary navigation. The exercises included in this book, as they are based on service methods and procedure, should be an easy and sure path to this end.

The practice of using ruler, set square and protractor for measuring courses, bearings etc. in the various exercises throughout the book may call for criticism. The instrument which is used invariably in the Royal Navy is the parallel ruler, and angles are measured directly from the true rose printed on all marine charts.

In consideration of the difficulty to-day in obtaining parallel rulers, the alternative, of set square and ruler, has perforce to be accepted. Where the parallel ruler is available it should always be used and, to obtain accurate readings, the dead centre of the rose should be marked by a short parallel through 270°–090° (west–east) cutting the 000°–180° meridian.

The authors are again indebted to the Admiralty for generous help and advice, particularly to Vice-Admiral J. G. P. Vivian, C.B., Admiral Commanding Reserves, to Instructor-Commander H. A. McDonald, B.Sc., R.N., and to Instructor-Commander E. I. Spinks, B.A., F.R.Met.Soc., R.N., who not only examined the book in manuscript, but offered helpful criticism based upon their wide experience. Sincere thanks are also extended to the Hydrographer of the Navy and to the Controller of H.M. Stationery Office for permission to use the practice chart included in the book.

S. A. W.

J. C. H.

September 1943

ELEMENTARY
MARINE NAVIGATION

INTRODUCTION

Navigation may be described as the art of conducting a vessel safely from one place on the earth's surface to another.

From the earliest times, when man first ventured upon the sea in ships, the spirit of adventure has urged him to try to discover what lies beyond the distant horizon.

For many long years the greatest obstacle to any voyage of discovery was the difficulty of finding one's way upon the open ocean, and few sailors in those days strayed far from the sight of land.

They knew enough to be able to steer an approximate course from the position of the sun by day and the stars by night, but an overcast sky would often rob them of even these rather hazardous guides. From remote ages, probably two or three thousand years ago, it was known that there was a certain black mineral, first discovered at Magnesia in Asia Minor (whence comes the name *magnet*), which had strange properties. It would exert a distinct "pull" upon any iron object, and if a length of this mineral were suspended by a string and allowed to come to rest of its own accord, it would set itself always in a direction north and south. Apparently it did not occur to anyone to make use of this valuable peculiarity of lodestone (leading stone), as it was called, until early in the fourteenth century. An Italian sailor, at Naples, then fitted strips of lodestone to the underside of a circular compass card, balanced at its centre, and originated what was probably the fore-runner of every mariner's compass. It is historically interesting to know that, for some reason, in honour of the Duke of Anjou, he labelled the north point of his card with the *fleur-de-lys*, and this practice has been handed down so that, even to-day, it is customary to mark the north point of a mariner's compass card with this device.

In spite, however, of all their handicaps and hazards, in spite of their lack of navigating instruments such as we possess to-day, in spite of having only their instincts and weather-wise experience as their "barometer", the extent of their navigation was surprisingly wide, and it is a credit to their industry and ingenuity that so much of what was recorded on their charts has been found, in later years, to be reliable.

THE PRINCIPLES OF NAVIGATION

To be successful a navigator must know many things, but the two most important are (1) direction, (2) distance. Direction is nearly always obtained by means of the *ship's compass* (which is described later), and the distance to be sailed is calculated from measurements in nautical miles on a marine chart.

There are four methods used for determining a ship's position at any time when at sea. These are (1) dead reckoning, (2) estimated position, (3) a "fix", which is determined by observation of fixed objects on the earth (terrestrial objects), (4) an observed position, which is obtained by calculation from the observed positions of heavenly bodies.

The first method is based upon calculating, or reckoning, the ship's position by knowing the direction in which the ship is heading (called the ship's *course*) and the speed of the ship.

The second method makes allowance for any estimated helpful, or adverse, effects of currents, tidal streams, and wind (leeway).

The third and fourth methods, which are by far the most important and accurate, make use of what are known as *position lines*. A position line is a line, straight or curved, drawn upon a chart so that the navigator's position is represented as being somewhere on that line. It follows, therefore, that if a navigator can, at the same time, plot on a chart two or more position lines, which cross one another, then his position must be represented as the intersection of these position lines.

To obtain a reliable reading of the ship's position the angle at which the position lines cross (known as the "angle of cut") should be never less than about 30°. The nearer it is to 90° the better, so that the effect of any small error in taking the observations and transferring them to the chart is reduced to a minimum.

Position lines may be of three kinds:

(*a*) Visual directions of terrestrial fixed objects.
(*b*) Wireless telegraph directions (w/t–d/f).
(*c*) Astronomical position lines.

(*a*) Suppose that a navigator in a ship at sea recognises an object on land in a direction due east of the ship. (This object is said to *bear* due east, or in other words, the *bearing* of the object from the ship is due east. Alternatively the bearing of the ship from the object is due west.)

A line drawn on a marine chart of this neighbourhood due *west* from this object provides a position line, somewhere along which the ship's position is represented.

If, at the same time, the bearing of, say, a lightship of known identity is due south, then a line drawn on the chart due north from this lightship is a second position line. The point of intersection represents the ship's position and constitutes a fix.

(*b*) A w/t–d/f position line is obtained from the wireless bearing of a radio station the position of which is known but which is beyond the range of vision. The bearing so obtained, after making a small necessary correction, is plotted as before through the position of the radio station on the chart. Another bearing, taken at the same time, of a different station provides the second position line and the fix.

(c) Navigation by astronomical position lines (observed position) is the most useful and important of all methods, and although the technicalities of astro-navigation are outside the design of this book, the principles upon which it is based may prove of interest. Every astronomical body in the heavens has, at any given moment, its *geographical position* on the earth. By this is meant that if a straight line is drawn from the centre of the earth to any astronomical body, then the point where that line passes through the earth's surface is called the geographical position of that body.

The actual position in the heavens (the celestial position) of the more important stars, the planets, the sun or the moon, is obtained at any time by reference to the Nautical Almanac, and from this position can be determined the corresponding geographical position of any chosen body. To obtain a position line a certain star or planet (or the sun or moon) is selected and its altitude above the horizontal plane is measured accurately with a sextant. By mathematical calculation the observer can then determine his actual distance from the geographical position of this body. If a navigator knows his distance from a fixed point it follows that his position line must be the circumference of a circle, with the fixed point as centre and the distance as radius. These "position circles" are usually so large that the small portion with which he is concerned may be plotted by a navigator on to a chart as a *straight* line, without any appreciable error. The reading of the altitude of a second celestial body provides a second position line, and the point of intersection of the two lines is the ship's "observed position".

Whenever possible, alternative methods should be employed for determining or checking position, both for purposes of practice and to give confidence in the accuracy of the calculation.

GEOMETRICAL PRINCIPLES USED IN NAVIGATION

Navigation mainly depends for its accuracy upon the correct estimation of distances and the careful reading of angles, so that it is imperative that a would-be navigator should be competent in the use of such geometrical instruments as will enable him to make accurate measurement.

These instruments are the ruler, compasses or dividers, set squares, parallel ruler (if available) and the protractor.

Accuracy must be a first consideration at all times, because any error in measurements taken from comparatively small-scale drawings or charts will become a very considerable discrepancy when magnified into distances of "real life".

There may often be several ways of performing a simple geometrical operation, but there is usually one way which is more accurate than the others.

For example, a line may be divided into two equal parts (bisected) by measuring its length with a ruler and halving this measurement to find the required length. It is more accurate to use compasses, as shown later.

When the length of a line has to be transferred from one position to another, it should always be marked off (if not too long) by using compasses rather than a ruler.

The above list of geometrical instruments will need no description here, with the possible exception of the circular protractor. This instrument, as used in navigation, is described on p. 20.

SOME SIMPLE GEOMETRICAL CONSTRUCTIONS

(a) Straight Lines and Angles.

1. *To bisect any given straight line of unknown length* (Fig. 1).

Let *AB* be the given straight line. On the point *A* place the point of the compasses open to any distance greater than half the length of *AB*. Describe an arc *CD*. With the compasses open to the *same* distance and the point upon *B* describe a second arc cutting the first at *E* and *F*. Join *E*, *F* by a straight line cutting the line *AB* at *G*. Then *AB* is bisected at the point *G*, so that *AG* is equal in length to *GB*, as may be tested with dividers.

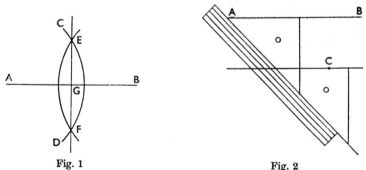

Fig. 1   Fig. 2

2. *Through any given point to draw a line parallel to a given straight line* (Fig. 2).

The method employed, using a set square and ruler, is illustrated in the diagram, where *AB* is the given straight line and *C* the given point.

3. *To draw a straight line perpendicular to a given straight line from any point within the given line* (Fig. 3).

This may be done by using a ruler and set square, by protractor, or by compasses. The last method is shown in Fig. 3. Let *AB* be the given straight line and *C* any point within it. With *C* as centre and any convenient radius describe arcs cutting *AB* in *D* and *E*. Proceed as in Fig. 1 to bisect the line *DE* and to draw the straight line *FG* which is perpendicular to *AB* at the point *C*.

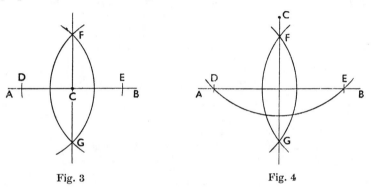

Fig. 3   Fig. 4

4. *To draw a straight line perpendicular to a given straight line from any point outside it* (Fig. 4).

This also can be done by methods similar to Fig. 3. Let *AB* be the given straight line and *C* any point outside it. With *C* as centre and any convenient radius describe an arc cutting *AB* in *D* and *E*. Proceed as in Fig. 1 to bisect *DE* and draw *CG* perpendicular to *AB* from the point *C*.

5. *To "copy" a given angle* (Fig. 5).

Let *ABC* be the angle it is required to copy. Draw any straight line *DE*. With *D* as centre and any convenient radius describe an arc cutting *DE* at *F*. With *B* as centre and the same radius draw a similar arc cutting *BA* and *BC* at *G* and *H* respectively. Open the compasses to the distance *HG* and with that radius and centre *F* cut the first arc at *J*. Join *JD*. The angle *JDE* is then equal to the angle *ABC*.

The above construction may, of course, be done by using a protractor, but the risk of error is then greater.

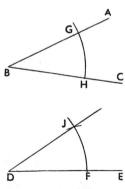

Fig. 5

6. *To bisect a given angle* (Fig. 6).

Let *ABC* be the given angle. With centre *B* and any convenient radius describe the arc *DE*. With centres *D* and *E* in turn draw two more arcs of equal radius to cut at *F*. Join *BF*. The angle *ABC* is then bisected by the line *BF*, so that the angle *ABF* is equal to the angle *FBC*.

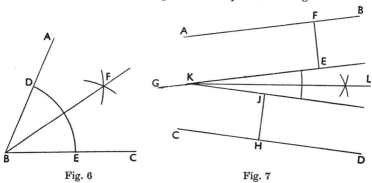

Fig. 6   Fig. 7

7. *To bisect the angle between two converging straight lines which do not intersect* (Fig. 7).

When two straight lines are not parallel they are said to converge. Let *AB* and *CD* be the two straight lines converging towards *A* and *C*, such that it is not convenient to produce them to the point of intersection. From any point *E*, within the two lines, draw *EF* perpendicular to *AB*, and *EG* parallel to *AB*. From any point *H*, in the line *CD*, draw a line perpendicular to *CD* and mark off a length *HJ* equal to *EF*. Through *J* draw *JK* parallel to *CD*, meeting the line *EG* at *K*. Bisect the angle *EKJ* by the line *KL*. Then if *BA*, *LK* and *DC* were produced they would all meet at the same point and *LK* would bisect the angle.

8. *Through any given point, within two converging straight lines, to draw a straight line which would pass through the point of intersection* (Fig. 8).

Let *AB* and *CD* be the converging straight lines and *E* the given point within them. Draw any straight line *FG* cutting *AB* and *CD*. Join *FE* and *GE*. From any convenient point *H*, in *AB*, draw *HJ* parallel to *FG*. From *H* draw a line parallel to *FE*, and from *J* a line parallel to *GE*, meeting at the point *K*. Join *EK*. Then *EK*, if produced, would pass through the intersection of the converging lines.

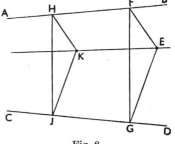

Fig. 8

9. *To find a point, in a given straight line, which is equidistant from two other points not in the line* (Figs. 9 and 9 *a*).

Let *AB* be the given straight line and *C* and *D* the two given points (on the same side of *AB* in Fig. 9, and on opposite sides in Fig. 9 *a*). Join *CD*. Bisect *CD* and produce the bisecting line (if necessary) to cut *AB* at *E*. Then *E* is the required point and the distance *EC* is equal to the distance *ED*, as may be checked by the dividers.

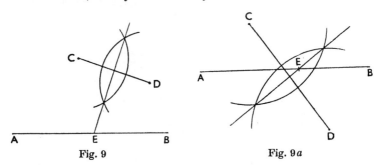

Fig. 9   Fig. 9 *a*

(*b*) The Circle.

The boundary line of any circle is called its *circumference* and every point on that circumference is equidistant from the centre by a distance called the *radius* of the circle.

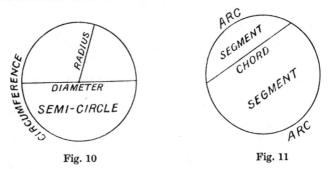

Fig. 10   Fig. 11

A straight line joining any two points on the circumference is called a *chord* of the circle and that portion of the circumference, between any two points on it, is an *arc*.

The longest chord of a circle is its *diameter*, which passes through the centre of the circle and divides it into two equal parts or *semicircles*.

The diameter of a circle is obviously equal in length to twice the radius.

That part of a circle bounded by a chord and an arc is called a *segment* of the circle.

A semicircle is a segment.

That portion of a circle bounded by two radii and an arc is known as a sector. If the radii are at right angles (90°) the sector is called a *quadrant* and four quadrants form a complete circle.

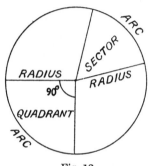

Fig. 12

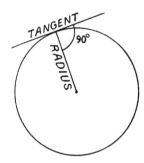

Fig. 13

A *tangent* to a circle is a straight line which touches the circumference at a point but which does not cut the circumference. It touches at the *point of contact* and is at right angles to the radius drawn to that point (Figs. 10–13).

10. *To find the centre of a circle* (Fig. 14).

Select any three points *A*, *B* and *C* on the circumference. Bisect each of the chords *AB* and *BC*. The point of intersection, *O*, of the two bisectors is the centre of the circle. This method may be applied to an arc of a circle when it is required to complete the circle of which the arc is part. Another problem, employing the same method, is to draw a circle through any three given points.

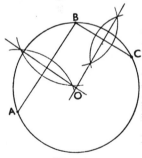

Fig. 14

11. *Angles in a segment of a circle* (Fig. 15).

Let *AB* be a chord of a circle dividing the circle into two segments. All angles in the same segment are equal, so that the angle *ACB* is equal to the angle *ADB*, and the angle *AEB* is equal to the angle *AFB*. In any segment less than a semicircle all the angles are *obtuse* (i.e. greater than a right angle). In any segment greater than a semicircle all the angles are *acute* (i.e. less than a right angle). In a semicircle all the angles are *right angles*, so that this affords a useful method of constructing a right angle (Fig. 16).

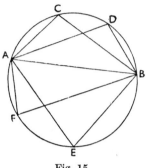

Fig. 15

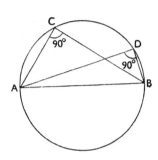

Fig. 16

12. *To draw a tangent to a given circle from a given point outside it* (Fig. 17).

Let *P* be the given point and *C* the centre of the given circle. Join *PC* and bisect it at the point *A*. With centre *A* and radius *AC* draw a circle to cut the given circle at *B* and *D*. Join *PB* and *PD*. Then *PB* and *PD* are tangents to the given circle.

13. *To draw a circle to pass through two given points and also to touch a given straight line* (Fig. 18).

This problem, in particular, has many useful applications in navigation.

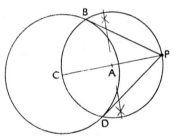

Fig. 17

Let *A* and *B* be the two given points and *CD* the given straight line. Join *BA* and bisect it. Produce *BA* to cut the line *CD* at *E*. Draw any circle through *A* and *B*, and from *E* draw a tangent, *ET*, to this circle. With centre *E* and radius *ET* describe an arc to cut *CD* at *F*. At *F* draw *FO* perpendicular to *CD*, cutting the bisection of *AB* at *O*. Then *O* is the centre of the circle that will pass through the points *A* and *B* and touch the line *CD* at *F*.

(*c*) **Scales.**

When solving a navigational problem graphically (by drawing) it is sometimes necessary to construct a suitably reduced scale of length applicable to the particular problem. In this connection the following problem is continually recurring.

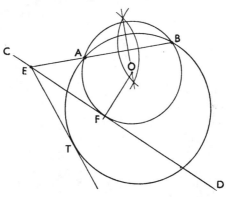

Fig. 18

14. *To divide a given straight line into any required number of equal parts* (Figs. 19 and 20).

Method 1. Let *AB* be the given straight line which it is required to divide into, say, five equal parts (Fig. 19). From *A* draw a straight line *AC* at any convenient angle to *AB*. From *A*, along *AC*, mark off, with compasses, five equal divisions numbered 1 to 5 as in the diagram. Join the number 5 mark to the point *B*. Through the numbers 4, 3, 2 and 1, draw lines parallel to *B*5. These parallel lines divide *AB* into five equal parts.

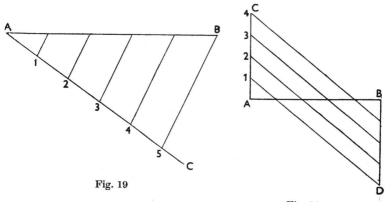

Fig. 19

Fig. 20

Method 2. Should the straight line *AB* be of short length, it is better to adopt the following method (Fig. 20). At *A* draw *AC* perpendicular to *AB* and at *B* draw *BD* perpendicular to *AB* but on the opposite side of it. Mark off *four* equal divisions, 1–4, along *AC* and four more of the same equal divisions along *BD*. Join these, as shown, and the line *AB* is then divided into five equal parts.

15. *To construct a diagonal scale.*

It is often necessary to measure the length of a line to a greater degree of accuracy than can be done by means of the ordinary ruler. For this purpose a diagonal scale should be used (Fig. 21). With a ruler and set square draw a rectangle 4 in. long by 1 in. high, and draw perpendiculars at 1 in. intervals as shown.

This will divide the rectangle into four 1 in. squares.

Divide one of these perpendiculars into 10 equal parts (i.e. each division is $\frac{1}{10}$ in.). From each of these divisions draw lines parallel to the base as shown.

Divide the top and bottom lines of the right-hand square also into $\frac{1}{10}$ths of an inch. Join these "diagonally", as in the diagram, and label the scale with the figures indicated.

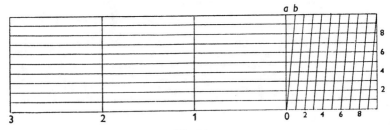

Fig. 21

This scale will then measure accurately to one hundredth of an inch (0·01 in.).

This will be readily understood if we consider the triangle *Oab*. The distance from the 3 in. mark to the point *O*, along the bottom horizontal line, is obviously 3 in. The distance from the 3 in. mark to the point *b*, along the top horizontal line, is 3·1 in., since *ab* = 0·1 in.

We know that the ten horizontal lines are spaced at intervals of $\frac{1}{10}$ in., so that the length from the 3 in. mark along the first horizontal to the intersection with the diagonal *Ob* is $3 + (\frac{1}{10}$ of 0·1) in. = 3·01 in.

The distance from the 3 in. mark along the number 2 horizontal to its intersection with the diagonal *Ob* is $3 + (\frac{2}{10}$ of 0·1) in. = 3·02 in., and so on.

To measure a length equal to 2·64 in. place the point of the compasses on the point of intersection of the number 6 "diagonal" with the number 4 horizontal. Open the compasses along the number 4 horizontal to the 2 in. mark. The distance thus measured is 2·64 in.

To measure a line of unknown length, first determine its approximate length with a ruler. If greater than 4 in. (since this is the maximum measurement we can make directly with the diagonal scale as drawn in Fig. 21) mark off a whole number of inches, by the ruler, so that the remainder is less than 4 in. Suppose, for example, that the line is more than 8 in. long, then mark off 5 in. by ruler, leaving between 3 and 4 in. to be measured.

Open the compasses accurately over this remaining length and with the point on the 3 in. mark of the diagonal scale determine which "intersection" agrees with the measured distance. If the agreement is along the number 7 horizontal at the intersection with the number 5 "diagonal", then the length measured is 3·57 in., and the length of the line in question is $5 + 3·57 = 8·57$ in.

16. *To construct a scale of ¾ in. = 1 foot, to show an accuracy of inches* (Fig. 22).

Draw a line 3 in. long and divide it into four equal parts each ¾ in. in length. Each division then represents 1 foot on the required scale. Number these, as shown, and subdivide the first division into 12 equal parts to represent individual inches.

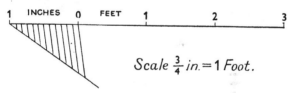

Fig. 22

17. *To construct a scale suitable for use with a chart whose scale is 1:1,000,000, to show accuracy to 1 nautical mile (2000 yd.)* (Fig. 23).

The scale of the chart is 1 in. represents 1,000,000 in., and since 1 nautical mile = 2000 yd. = 72,000 in., the scale is 1 in. represents

$$\frac{1,000,000}{72,000} \text{ nautical miles, i.e. } 13·9 \text{ nautical miles.}$$

If we divide the scale into sections of 10 nautical miles, the length of the line representing this distance is found thus:

13·9 nautical miles is represented by 1 in.

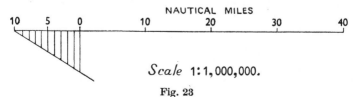

Fig. 23

Therefore 10 nautical miles is represented by

$$\frac{10}{13 \cdot 9}, \quad \text{i.e. } 0 \cdot 72 \text{ in.}$$

By means of the diagonal scale, divide a line into lengths of 0·72 in., each representing 10 nautical miles, and subdivide the left-hand section into 10 equal parts to show individual nautical miles.

(*d*) The Circular Protractor.

This instrument is used for measuring angles and for the construction of angles of any required dimension. The protractor shown in Fig. 24 is made of transparent celluloid or plastic and the scale is graduated in degrees (and half degrees if the protractor is large enough) extending from true north (000°) through a complete circle of 360° back to north again.

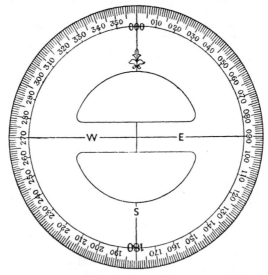

Fig. 24

Cross hair-line diameters, at right angles, from 000° to 180°, and from 090° to 270°, are etched so that their intersection is the exact centre of the circle making up the scale.

18. *To measure an angle with the protractor.*

Let *ABC* (Fig. 25) be the angle to be measured. Place the centre of the protractor (the intersection of the cross-lines) exactly on the point *B*, with the north line (000°) of the protractor coinciding with the line *BA*. Then the line *BC* will be found to coincide with the graduation 104°, and this is the value of the angle in degrees. It is sometimes necessary to extend the length of the lines *BA* and *BC* to "fit" the protractor. This must be done as carefully and as accurately as possible.

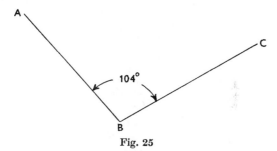

Fig. 25

True Course, True Bearing and True Track.

The circular protractor is used for laying off or measuring true courses, bearings and tracks which are always measured in degrees from true north (000°) in a clockwise direction. A ship's track is her direction of motion relative to sea bottom and, because of ocean currents, wind effects, etc., it may be different from her course. To avoid confusion true courses, bearings and tracks are always expressed in "three-figure" notation, i.e. initial zeros are added where necessary to complete the three digits. For example, a true course of 4° is written 004°.

EXERCISE 1.

1. Using only compasses, ruler and set square, copy this line of soundings to a scale three-quarters of its present measurement. '

FATHOMS

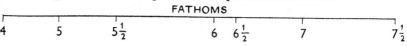

2. Construct a scale for use with a chart whose scale is 1:100,000 to show an accuracy of 1 cable (200 yd.).

3. Construct a scale of 5 in. = 1 cable, in sections of 50 yd., to show accuracy to 1 fathom.

4. The navigator of a vessel, from a certain position at sea, observes a church and a windmill to be in line. The ship is 5 nautical miles to seaward from the church and 9 nautical miles from the windmill, and the bearing of the two objects from the ship is 055°. The ship's track is 086°. Using a scale of 1 in. = 1 nautical mile, find by drawing to scale:

(*a*) How far the ship must steam before she is equidistant from the church and the windmill.

(*b*) Her distance from each object at that time.

(*c*) The bearing of each object from the ship at that time.

5. Fig. 26 represents a ship's derrick plumbing a hatch. Construct a scale of 1 in. = 10 ft., and use it to draw the figure to scale. From it find:

(*a*) The length of the derrick pendant.

(*b*) The inclination of the derrick to the vertical.

(*c*) The distance of the fall from the foot of the mast if the derrick pendant is made 30 ft. long.

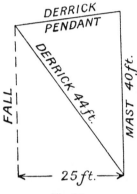

Fig. 26

6. The stellar constellation known as the GREAT BEAR contains seven stars named, respectively, Dubhe, Merak, Phecda, Megrez, Alioth, Mizar and Benetnasch. The pole star itself is called Polaris. On a sheet of drawing paper, near the top right-hand corner, place a point to represent Polaris. Due south of this position and at a distance of 11·8 cm. plot the position of Dubhe.

From the following measurements, all of which are in centimetres, plot the whole constellation and insert the name of each star as its position is established: Benetnasch to Polaris 17·0; Benetnasch to Dubhe 11·0; Merak south of Dubhe 2·2; Merak to Benetnasch 11·1; Phecda to Merak 3·4; Dubhe south-westwards to Phecda 4·3; Megrez in a northerly direction from Phecda 1·9; Megrez to Dubhe 4·2; Megrez to Alioth 2·4; Alioth to Phecda 3·9; Mizar to Alioth 2·0; Phecda to Mizar 5·7.

Plot the position of the true celestial north pole on this diagram, given that it is 16·5 from Benetnasch and 11·3 from Dubhe. What is its distance, to the same scale, from Polaris?

7. A ship is steaming in a circle of radius 3 nautical miles. The centre of this circle is 10 nautical miles south-west of a lighthouse which is visible. What is the greatest and the least bearing of the lighthouse from the ship as it steams in its circle?

8. A light *A* is 10 miles north-east of a light *B*. A third light, *C*, is in a south-easterly direction 11 miles from *B* and 12·5 miles from *A*. A ship's course takes it through a point equidistant from these three lights. How far is the vessel from each light at that moment?

9. A ship is steaming in a direction 025° and a light is observed to Port, bearing 355° from the ship and distant 5 nautical miles.

(*a*) What is the angle between the ship's fore and aft line and the direction of the light?

(*b*) How far will the vessel steam before this angle is doubled?

(*c*) What will be the bearing of the light when the ship has reached this position?

(*d*) What will be the ship's nearest distance from the light as she proceeds along her course?

10. The bearing of a lighthouse *B* is 108° from another lighthouse *A*, and they are 16 nautical miles apart. If the light from *A* is visible from a distance of 10 nautical miles, and the light from *B* from a distance of 8 nautical miles, what is the greatest distance in a straight line that a ship can steam with both lights visible, and in what direction will she be steering?

11. A mooring buoy is anchored to sea bottom in 8 fathoms of water, with a mooring chain 60 ft. long. A vessel 72 ft. long is moored to the buoy with 10 ft. of cable between the ship's stem and the buoy. Assuming all cables to be taut, find the radius of swing of the ship's stern from the point vertically above the mooring point of the buoy.

12. *A*, *B* and *C* are three prominent objects on shore such that *AC* = 10·5 miles; *AB* = 5·9 miles; *BC* = 4·9 miles. *B* is to seaward of the line joining *A* and *C*. A vessel offshore finds the angle between her position and the objects *A* and *B* to be 51° and the similar angle between *B* and *C* to be 54°. Using the method of "angles in a segment" construct the ship's position and state how far she is from the objects *A* and *C* respectively.

THE FORM OF THE EARTH

Terms and Definitions.

For all navigational purposes the earth is generally assumed to be a perfect sphere.

The *axis* of the earth (*NS* in Fig. 27) is that diameter about which the earth performs its daily rotation in approximately 24 hours of mean solar time.

The *poles* of the earth are the extremities of this axis, and that pole nearer to the Pole Star is called the North Pole of the earth (N.). The opposite pole is the South Pole (S.).

The *equator* (EQ.) is that circle drawn upon the earth's surface such that every point on its circumference is equidistant from both the north and south poles.

A *great circle* drawn upon the earth is any circle the centre of which is the centre also of the earth. The equator is a great circle. If two points on the earth's surface are at opposite ends of the same diameter, then an infinite number of great circles may be drawn through them. If the two points are not diametrically opposite then only one great circle can be drawn through them. The shortest distance between any two places on the earth's surface is the smaller arc of the great circle that joins them.

A *small circle* drawn upon the earth is any circle whose centre does not coincide with the centre of the earth.

A *meridian* is any one of the infinite number of semi-great circles that can be drawn through the north and south poles of the earth.

The position of any point on the earth is defined in terms of *latitude* and *longitude*, the latitude being always given first, followed by the longitude. The latitude of any place may be defined as the angle subtended at the earth's centre by the arc of the meridian intercepted between that place and the equator. Thus the latitude of A (Fig. 27) is the angle $A'OA$. Latitude is measured from the equator, north or south, from 0° to 90°, to an accuracy of degrees, minutes and seconds.

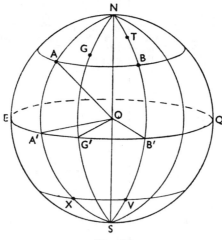

Fig. 27

It follows that there can be an infinite number of points on the earth's surface with the same latitude and these will form a small circle whose plane is parallel to that of the equator, and called a *parallel of latitude*. The longitude of any place is measured east or west from the *zero* or *prime* meridian, which is the meridian passing through Greenwich (G in Fig. 27). It is the angle subtended at the earth's centre by the shorter arc of the equator intercepted between the prime meridian and the meridian at that place. So that the longitude of T is the angle $G'OB'$ east, and the longitude of A is the angle $G'OA'$ west.

Difference of latitude (d.lat.) between any two places is the arc of any meridian intercepted between the latitude parallels of those two places.

Thus the d.lat. between A and V (Fig. 27) is the arc $AA'X$. It is termed north or south according to the direction of the change. If the two places are on the same side of the equator its magnitude is obtained by subtracting the respective latitudes. If on opposite sides of the equator the d.lat. is obtained by adding the respective latitudes.

Difference of Longitude (d.long.) between any two places is the shorter arc of the equator intercepted between the meridians of the two places. Thus in Fig. 27 d.long. between A and V is the arc $A'G'B'$. It is termed east or west according to the direction of the change. If the longitudes are both of the same kind (i.e. both east or both west) the d.long. is obtained by subtracting the respective longitudes. If of opposite kinds, the d.long. is the sum of the longitudes.

The sum of two longitudes of opposite kind may sometimes exceed 180°, but since a d.long. can never have an actual value of more than 180° E. or W., the result should be subtracted from 360° and the direction of the change should be reversed (see Example II).

EXAMPLE I. What is the d.lat. and d.long. between point A (lat. 41° 32′ N., long. 05° 42′ E.) and point B (lat. 24° 46′ N., long. 56° 38′ E.)?

	Latitude	Longitude
A	41° 32′ N.	05° 42′ E.
B	24° 46′ N.	56° 38′ E.
d.lat.	16° 46′ S.	d.long. 50° 56′ E.

EXAMPLE II. Find the d.lat. and d.long. from point F (31° 24′ S., 118° 31′ E.) to point T (25° 13′ N., 96° 18′ W.).

	Latitude	Longitude
F	31° 24′ S.	118° 31′ E.
T	25° 13′ N.	96° 18′ W.
d.lat.	56° 37′ N.	d.long. 214° 49′ W.

Since the d.long (214° 49′ W.) exceeds 180° it is subtracted from 360° and the direction reversed.

Thus the d.long. is (360° − 214° 49′) E. = 145° 11′ E.

The nautical mile. The length of any small arc of a meridian that subtends an angle of one minute at the earth's centre is called a nautical mile. In other words a nautical mile is one minute of latitude. Its value varies slightly in different latitudes because the earth is not a perfect sphere, but the usually accepted length of a nautical mile is 6080 ft. The round figure of 6000 ft. (2000 yd.) is generally used for ranging purposes. The abbreviation for nautical mile is n.m. or ′ (the symbol representing one minute). Fractions of a nautical mile are usually expressed as decimals and it is customary to place the symbol immediately in front of the decimal point, e.g. 25·3 nautical miles is written 25′·3. A speed of one nautical mile per hour is called a *knot*.

A *rhumb line* drawn upon the earth's surface is a line so drawn that it cuts every meridian it crosses at the same angle. The firm line AB (Fig. 28) is a rhumb line since all the angles θ are of the same magnitude. Parallels of latitude are special examples of rhumb lines, where the angle at which they cut the meridians is always a right angle.

The dotted line *AB* represents the great circle distance between *A* and *B* and consequently it is shorter than the rhumb line distance from *A* to *B*. The advantage of steering a rhumb line track from *A* to *B* is that the ship's course is constant, apart from current effects, if any, whereas a ship steering a great circle course from *A* to *B* would be continually

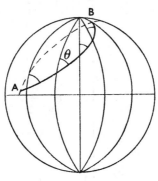

Fig. 28

"under helm". For distances up to 1000 nautical miles the rhumb line track is only slightly longer than the great circle track, but for long runs the difference may be considerable. When steering a long run on a great circle track it is usual to steer a sequence of rhumb line tracks between points which are actually on the great circle.

Mercator's Chart.

So far all the explanations and details given have been considered from reference to the earth as a sphere. This arrangement, from the point of view of practical navigation and representation of details of the various areas of the earth's surface, is very inconvenient. It is obviously of much greater advantage to have this information printed on a flat surface. Since the earth is spherical it is impossible to represent any connected portion of its area on a plane surface without distortion. If a perfect map or chart could be made then all areas on the earth would be represented by exactly similar areas on the map. Since this cannot be done the only alternative is to sacrifice some less important features so as to preserve the correctness of the more important.

For purposes of navigation the most important considerations in the construction of a chart are:

(1) All rhumb lines (as just defined) must be straight lines.

(2) All angles on the earth's surface must be represented by exactly similar angles on the chart.

When these two conditions are observed, it follows that courses, tracks and bearings may be laid down and measured on such a chart simply by using a parallel ruler or a ruler and protractor (see preface).

Obviously, since a rhumb line on a Mercator's chart is a straight line, and since it cuts all meridians it crosses at the same angle, then meridians on a Mercator's chart must be represented by parallel straight lines all pointing north and south.

Similarly, parallels of latitude (which themselves are rhumb lines cutting the meridians at right angles) must be parallel straight lines pointing east and west.

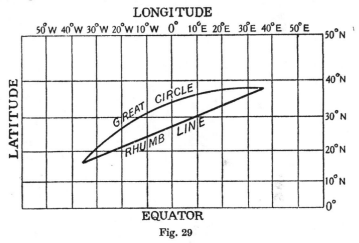

Fig. 29

We know that the shortest distance between any two points on the earth's surface is the great circle arc which joins them, but on a Mercator's chart it appears as though the rhumb line is the shortest distance. Because of this peculiarity, sizes of continents and distances between places should not be compared by eye (Fig. 29).

Let us now examine the small Mercator chart provided. The parallel of latitude 50° N. is shown and a scale of minutes of latitude is given in both the left- and right-hand borders. The meridians of longitude 4° W., 5° W. and 6° W. also are indicated, with a scale of minutes of longitude in both the top and bottom borders. To determine the latitude and longitude of any place or object, such as START POINT LIGHT, indicated on the chart by a black dot to represent the position of the light, place a set square along parallel 50° N. and with the aid of a ruler, as shown in Fig. 2 (p. 11), transfer the parallel through START POINT LIGHT. Draw a short length of this parallel to cut the latitude scale of the chart and read 50° 13½′ N.

In a similar manner draw a portion of the meridian through START POINT LIGHT, cutting the longitude scale, and read 3° 39′ W.

The position of START POINT LIGHT is therefore given as 50° 13½′ N., 3° 39′ W.

EXERCISE 2. From the chart read the latitude and longitude of the following objects.

Note. The centre of the black dot is to be regarded as the position of a light except in the case of light-vessels ⚓ or buoys ⚓, when the dot in the centre of the water line indicates the position. Work to the nearest half minute.

No.	Object	Latitude	Longitude
1.	Lizard Head Lt.		
2.	Pentire Pt.		
3.	Bishop Rock Lt.		
4.	Gribbin Head		
5.	Seven Stones ⚓		

Name the object charted in the following positions:

No.	Object	Latitude	Longitude
6.		50° 16½′ N.	3° 34′ W.
7.		50° 03′ N.	5° 01′ W.
8.		49° 57′ N.	5° 49′ W.
9.		50° 25½′ N.	5° 06′ W.
10.		50° 34′ N.	3° 46′ W.

Find the d.lat. and d.long. between the following pairs of objects, working from *F* to *T*.

No.	From *F*	To *T*
11.	Eddystone Lt.	Longships Lt.
12.	St Mary's Lt.	Berry Head Lt.
13.	St Anthony Pt. Lt.	Trevose Head Lt.
14.	Cape Cornwall W/T.O.	Start Pt. Lt.
15.	Trevose Head Lt.	Lizard Head Lt.

Distances on a Mercator's Chart.

All distances on a Mercator's marine chart must be measured in nautical miles (i.e. minutes of latitude) from the latitude scale provided.

The scale of longitude, in the top and bottom borders, must *never* be used for the determination of distance.

The charted length of a nautical mile on a Mercator's chart will be found, by comparison of the same distance on different parts of the latitude scale, to vary according to the latitude in which it is measured. It is not permissible therefore to use any portion of the latitude scale that we please. Only that part of the scale may be used which is in the latitudes of the distance to be measured. Suppose that we wish to determine the distance represented by the straight line *AB* (Fig. 30).

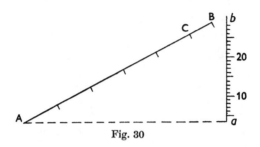

Fig. 30

The scale used must be obtained from the section *ab*, i.e. the scale used must be for nautical miles in the appropriate latitudes. Select, with dividers, a convenient distance (say 10 nautical miles) midway between *a* and *b*, and step this distance along *AB*, counting the number of 10 mile lengths so measured. Suppose that five of these lengths bring us to the point *C*, so that *CB* is less than 10 nautical miles.

With dividers open to the distance *CB* measure this downwards from *b* on the latitude scale. This length measures, say, 7 nautical miles. The total length represented by *AB* is, therefore, $5 \times 10 + 7 = 57$ nautical miles.

True Course on a Mercator's Chart.

A constant course, or direction, if there is no drift due to currents or tidal streams, is represented on a Mercator's chart by a rhumb line. This direction, when measured in degrees from the true meridian clockwise from 000° to 360°, is a *true* course.

On a chart this angle is measured either by protractor aligned along a true meridian, or more usually by transferring the rhumb line by parallel ruler, or set square, to pass through the centre of the true rose.

EXAMPLE. Suppose that a vessel has to steam from LIZARD HEAD LIGHT to EDDYSTONE LIGHT, assuming that there is no drift due to tidal stream, What true course must she steer?

First draw the rhumb line between LIZARD HEAD LIGHT and EDDYSTONE LIGHT, and transfer this by parallels through the centre of the true rose, cutting the scale at 069°. The true course, therefore, is 069°.

The return, or *reciprocal* true course, from EDDYSTONE LIGHT to LIZARD HEAD LIGHT, would be $069° + 180° = 249°$.

EXERCISE 3. From the chart determine the true course to steer, assuming no tidal drift, and measure the distance to be steamed.

Work always with a sharp pencil, drawing fine lines, to provide greater accuracy, and so that they may be easily removed without unnecessary damage to the chart.

No.	From	To	True course	Dis-tance
1.	Bishop Rock Lt.	Lizard Head Lt.		
2.	Seven Stones ⚓	5 n.m. north of Trevose Head Lt.		
3.	49° 32′ N., 6° 24′ W.	8 n.m. south of Eddystone Lt.		
4.	Longships Lt.	49° 25′ N., 4° 45′ W.		
5.	Prawle Pt.	49° 31′ N., 5° 34′ W.		
6.	49° 30′ N., 5° 00′ W.	Western end of Plymouth Breakwater		
7.	49° 44′ N., 3° 25′ W.	St Anthony Pt. Lt.		
8.	5 n.m. south of Start Pt. Lt.	20 n.m. south of Wolf Lt.		

9. How many nautical miles is Lizard Head Light from (a) the Equator, (b) the Greenwich Meridian?

The Clearing Circle.

A ship is sometimes required to steer a course so that she will "clear" an object by a given distance.

EXAMPLE. Suppose that a ship has to steer from position A to clear point B by 5 n.m.

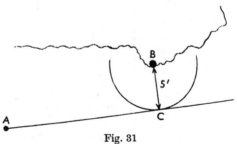

Fig. 31

With B as centre, and the chart distance of the clearance (5 n.m.) as radius, a clearing circle is drawn (Fig. 31). The tangent AC is then the course required.

When the vessel reaches the position C the object B is abeam to port, provided there is no tidal drift.

Notice particularly that this course is different from one passing 5 n.m. south of B.

Dead Reckoning (D.R.) Position.

As previously defined this position is determined by calculation of distance travelled on a known course, without any allowance for tidal stream, current, or wind effect. It should be recorded on the chart by a small +, with the time to which it refers, e.g. +D.R. 08 40.

When entering it in the log record it should be stated either in latitude and longitude, or as a true bearing and distance from a prominent object. Thus 130° Eddystone 10' indicates a position bearing 130° *from* EDDYSTONE LIGHT and distant 10 nautical miles along the line of bearing.

EXERCISE 4. Determine the latitude and longitude of the following positions:

No.	Bearing and distance	Latitude	Longitude
1.	275° Trevose Head Light 12'		
2.	187° Longships Light 14'		
3.	000° Seven Stones ⚓ 2'·5		
4.	195° Gribbin Head 7'·5		
5.	325° Wolf Light 9'		

State the true bearing and distance of the following charted positions from the named objects:

No.	Latitude	Longitude	Charted object	Bearing and distance
6.	50° 06' N.	3° 30' W.	Start Point Light	
7.	50° 20' N.	5° 42' W.	Godrevy Light	
8.	49° 49' N.	4° 55' W.	Manacles Bell Buoy	
9.	50° 15' N.	4° 04' W.	Mewstone	
10.	50° 03' N.	6° 43' W.	Bishop Rock Light	

EXERCISE 5. Plot on the chart the D.R. position at the times indicated.

No.	Position	Time of leaving	True course	Speed in knots	Time	D.R. position
1.	49° 43' N., 3° 40' W.	10 00	270°	12	14 00	Lat. and long.
2.	220° Wolf Lt. 10'	16 00	085°	15	20 30	Lat. and long.
3.	180° Start Pt. Lt. 8'	22 30	249°	13½	05 30	Lat. and long.
4.	50° 43½' N., 4° 55' W.	08 15	227°	16	11 15	Bearing and distance from Longships Lt.
5.	131° St Mary's Lt. 9'	15 48	078°	20	19 00	Bearing and distance from Eddystone Lt.

EXERCISE 6. In this exercise assume that there is no tidal stream.

1. At 08 00 hr. a ship was in position 50° 25′ N., 6° 11′ W., steaming on a true course of 158° at 12 knots. At 11 00 hr. course was altered to clear Lizard Head Lt. by 6′ and to leave it to port. Find (*a*) the D.R. position at 15 00 hr.; (*b*) the course after 11 00 hr.; (*c*) the time at which Lizard Head Lt. was abeam to port.

2. A vessel is steaming on a true course of 250° at 15 knots and at 15 30 hr. Eddystone Lt. is abeam to starboard at a distance of 7′. When Wolf Lt. bears 005°, from the vessel, course is altered to leave Seven Stones ⚓ 5′ on the port hand and speed is increased, at the same time, to 18 knots. Find (*a*) time of change of speed; (*b*) the new course; (*c*) D.R. position at 22 00 hr.

3. At 06 00 hr. a ship was in position 270° Pentire Pt. 10′, steaming at 16 knots on a true course of 221°. At 08 30 hr. course was altered to 150° and at 09 30 hr. speed was increased to 17 knots. At 10 30 hr. course was again altered and shaped for the western end of Plymouth Breakwater. Find (*a*) the D.R. position at 09 30 hr.; (*b*) the course after 10 30 hr.; (*c*) the speed to use after 10 30 hr. to arrive off the breakwater at 15 30 hr.

4. At 22 00 hr. a vessel was 8′ from Start Pt. Lt. and steering a course so that Start Pt. Lt. and Berry Head Lt. were in line and both dead astern. Her speed was 14 knots. Using the information on the chart, giving the visibility distance of the lights concerned, find (*a*) the time when Start Pt. Lt. should disappear from view, (*b*) the D.R. position at that time, (*c*) if, at that time, the ship's course is set straight for Eddystone Lt., at what time that flashing light should first be visible.

5. On the chart draw the seaward arc of visibility of Lizard Head Lt. At 00 00 hr. a vessel is in position 240° Eddystone Lt. 8′ steaming at 12 knots on a true course of 220°. Find (*a*) the time interval during which the Lizard Head Lt. is visible, (*b*) the time and distance of nearest approach to the light.

THE MAGNETIC COMPASS

Most of us are familiar with the pocket magnetic compass in which a small magnetic needle is suspended at its centre of gravity on a vertical pivot above a graduated compass card. This, with some very necessary improvements and adjustments, is the basis of the magnetic compass used for shaping and reading a ship's course at sea.

Before describing this instrument in detail it is perhaps as well to understand the forces that govern its movement.

Natural and Artificial Magnets.

As already mentioned in the introduction, it has been known for some thousands of years that a natural ore of iron has properties which enable it to attract to itself small pieces of iron and steel. Such a substance is known as a *natural magnet.*

It has also been discovered that these magnetic properties can be transferred to pieces of iron and steel when stroked in one direction (not backwards and forwards) by the magnetic ore. These pieces of iron or steel become *artificial magnets.*

When stroking a piece of soft, or pure, iron it is found that the magnetic properties are retained by the soft iron only while it is in close proximity to the magnetic ore. When removed it instantly loses magnetism. Such a magnet is known as a *temporary magnet.* The steel, on the other hand, retains its magnetism over a long period and is called a *permanent magnet.*

Magnets are not, of course, made to-day in this primitive manner, although the methods of making magnets are perhaps outside our immediate concern.

Properties of Magnets.

All magnets, whether natural or artificial, have similar properties. The attracting power of a magnet appears to be concentrated at definite regions near each end of the magnet, and these regions are called *poles.* These poles are not all alike as may be shown in this way. Allow two freely suspended bar magnets, at some·distance apart, to come to rest. They will, as we know, each point in a northerly and southerly direction. If we bring together the two ends which are pointing north they will repel each other, and so will the two ends pointing south. One north and one south end will attract each other. From these results we establish what is known as the first law of magnetism—*like poles repel each other, unlike poles attract each other.*

The Earth as a Magnet.

The earth itself is a huge spherical natural magnet with its poles situated near to, but unfortunately not exactly, true north and south, and it is this magnetic influence of the earth which controls the movement of the needle of a magnetic compass.

The needle, when at rest, sets itself in the plane of the earth's magnetic field at that place. In other words the compass needle sets itself in line with the *magnetic meridian* at that place, as distinct from the *true meridian.*

The Magnetic Compass.

The magnetic compass used for steering at sea consists of a compass card similar to the one shown in Fig. 32. In addition to the thirty-two main compass points the card is graduated from both north (0°) and south (0°) through 90° to both east and west. This latter system (compass notation) is now more favoured for steering than the older "point" system, and is described on p. 41.

Fig. 32

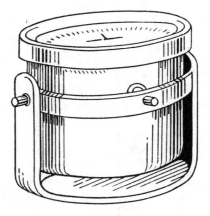

Fig. 33

On the under side of the card, and secured to it so as to be parallel to the north and south line of the card, is a "system" of six or eight short bar magnets spaced equally on either side of the pivot. The setting of the needles thus automatically sets the card as well.

A freely suspended compass system is a very sensitive instrument and if disturbed from its position of rest would take some time to settle down again. To overcome this oscillation the system is carried in a sealed bowl which is filled with liquid (usually a mixture which does not easily freeze, of alcohol and water) which, through friction, slows up the oscillation very considerably. This checking of the needle's sensitiveness is called *damping*.

The bowl itself is fixed in a stand called the *binnacle* and is suspended by *gimbals*, as shown in Fig. 33. This arrangement, as will be seen, prevents undue movement of the bowl out of the horizontal when the ship is rolling or pitching. The fore and aft line of the ship is indicated by the *lubber's point*, which projects from the inside of the bowl to the edge of the compass card.

Variation.

Because a compass needle, when undisturbed by outside influences other than the earth's magnetic force, sets itself along the magnetic meridian at any place, and not along the true meridian, it is at once obvious that a correction must be made to a compass reading before a *true* direction, i.e. one relative to true north, can be determined. The angle between the true meridian and the magnetic meridian at any place is called the *variation* at that place and is measured in degrees and minutes E. or W. of the true meridian, as the case may be.

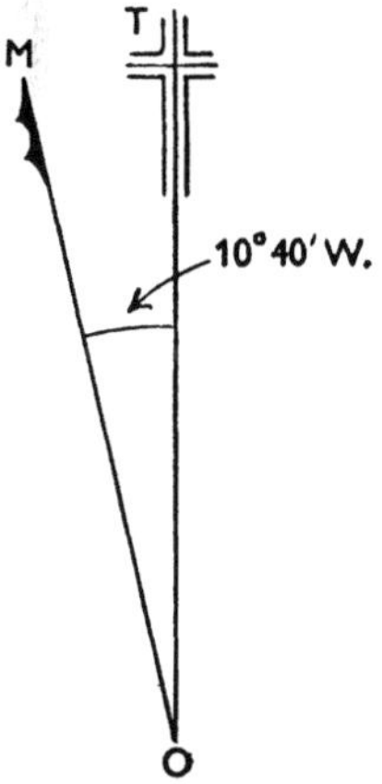

EXAMPLE. Suppose that at a place *O* the variation is 10° 40′ W. This means that the magnetic meridian at *O* is west of the true meridian by 10° 40′. Shown diagrammatically this could be represented as in Fig. 34, where *TO* is the true meridian and *MO* is the magnetic meridian. The angle *TOM* (10° 40′) is the variation, which is westerly.

It is shown quite clearly in Fig. 35 that variation differs for different places. If *T* and *M* are the true and magnetic north poles respectively, then the variation at *A* (angle *TAM*) is much less than the variation at *B* (angle *TBM*).

Not only is variation different at different places, it is not constant at any one place. The magnetic force of the earth is always slowly changing, but the change is very small and reasonably consistent, so that the change in variation, at any place, can be predicted over a period. All

10° 40′ W.

O

Fig. 34

charts used for navigation contain information as to the variation for that neighbourhood, together with the date of the magnetic survey. This appears inside the compass roses and upon dotted *isogonic lines* upon the chart. These are lines drawn to pass through all places on the chart that have the same variation. It is usual to draw them for each whole degree E. or W. The amount of yearly change and its direction is also recorded on the chart.

Thus "Variation 13° W. (1937) decreasing 12′ annually" means that the variation at that place in 1942 would be

$$13° - (5 \times 12') = 12° \text{ W.}$$

On the practice chart provided, the variation will be seen to be 13° W. and no date or mention of annual change is recorded.

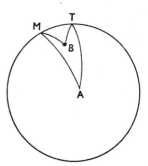

Fig. 35

Deviation.

All modern ships are built of iron and steel, and the hull of the ship when under construction is fixed in one position under the influence of the earth's magnetic field. This influence, which is increased by the hammering and riveting while the ship is being built, results in the hull becoming magnetised into a permanent, or semi-permanent, magnet.

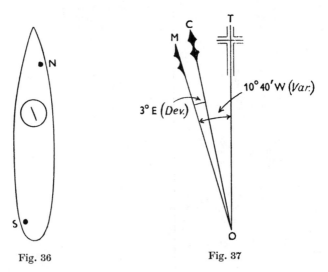

Fig. 36   Fig. 37

As we have seen, any magnet acts as though its attracting power is concentrated at its poles, so the ship, therefore, has a north pole and a south pole of its own.

Let us assume that a ship has a north pole in the starboard bow and a south pole in the port quarter (Fig. 36).

The compass, fitted as it usually is, a little to for'ard along the fore and aft line of the ship, will be influenced, not only by the earth's magnetic force, but also by the ship's own magnetism. The result of these two forces will most likely be that the needle will set itself not exactly in the magnetic meridian, but will be deflected by a few degrees from this position. This deflection is known as *deviation*, and it is measured, as in the case of variation, in degrees and minutes, but the measurement is E. or W. of the *magnetic* meridian, since it is from this meridian that the ship's magnetic force has deflected the needle. If we assume this amount of deviation to be 3° E., and apply it to the diagram in Fig. 34, we have the actual position of the compass needle as shown by *CO* in Fig. 37.

Deviation, as well as variation, is not constant and it depends upon the course on which the ship is heading.

For simplicity of explanation, let us adopt the usual conventional symbols for north and south poles. A north pole is generally referred to as a *red* pole and a south pole as a *blue* pole, but because the north magnetic pole of the earth attracts the north pole of a compass needle, the earth is assumed to have a *blue* pole in the north and a *red* pole in the south.

Referring again to the case of the ship in Fig. 36 with a red pole (*R*) in the starboard bow and a blue pole (*B*) in the port quarter, this ship is shown, in Fig. 38, heading in the directions of the eight main compass points.

As will at once be seen, the different positions of the ship's head, and the consequent alteration in the relative positions of the ship's poles and the poles of the compass needle, cause a different deviation of the compass for different headings. A study of Fig. 38 will make this quite clear.

Had the position of the ship's red and blue poles been different from that in Fig. 38, the resulting deviation would, naturally, have been different. The actual deviations are measured in degrees, and if large they are corrected so as to reduce them to not more than about 2°. This correction is accomplished by placing small permanent magnets (called compensator or corrector magnets) in lockers in the binnacle, provided for that purpose. It is never possible, however, to eliminate deviation on all courses, so the remaining deviations, after as many corrections as possible have been made, are recorded in the form of a deviation table. From the deviation table a deviation curve may be constructed and used if preferred. A typical deviation table and deviation curve are shown in Figs. 39 and 39 *a*. The deviation curve is easier to read than the deviation table and enables the deviation for intermediate courses to be quickly estimated.

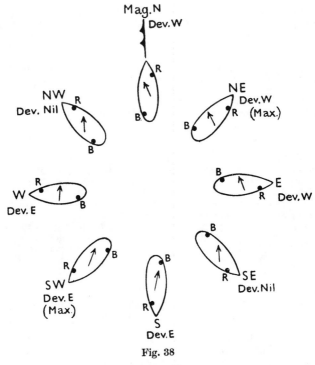

Fig. 38

DEVIATION TABLE

Ship's head by compass	Deviation
N.	1° W.
N. 30° E.	2° W.
N. 60° E.	2½° W.
E.	1½° W.
S. 60° E.	½° W.
S. 30° E.	½° E.
S.	1½° E.
S. 30° W.	2° E.
S. 60° W.	2° E.
W.	1½° E.
N. 60° W.	½° E.
N. 30° W.	½° W.
N.	1° W.

Fig. 39

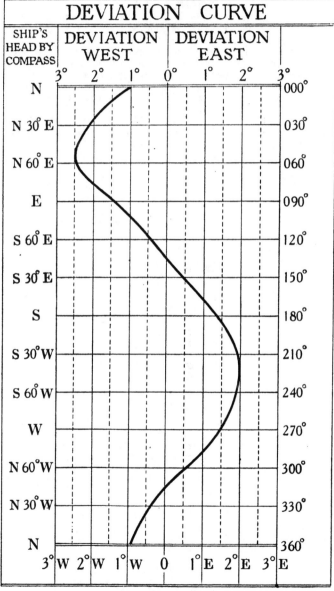

Fig. 39 a

Correction for Variation and Deviation.

EXAMPLE I. Suppose that a vessel is, say, 22 n.m. due south of BISHOP ROCK LIGHT and a course has to be shaped for EDDYSTONE LIGHT. It is assumed that there is no tidal drift.

The rhumb line drawn on the chart from the position 22 n.m. south of BISHOP ROCK LIGHT to EDDYSTONE LIGHT will, by measurement from the true meridian, give the true course to steer. This reads 064°.

Draw a true meridian *TA* (Fig. 40) and from *A* draw an angle *TAB* equal to 064°. Then *AB* will represent the ship's true course of 064°.

Because of the variation and deviation errors of the ship's compass, this is *not* the actual course that the helmsman has to shape. Let us assume that the variation in this region is 13° W., and draw, through *A*, the magnetic meridian *MA*, 13° west of *TA*.

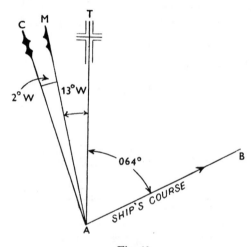

Fig. 40

We see at once that the corresponding *magnetic* course (i.e. the direction of the ship's head relative to the magnetic meridian) is 064° + 13° = 077°. If there were no deviation of the compass needle from the magnetic meridian, then this course of 077° would be the course to steer. But if we take the deviation table or curve (Figs. 39 and 39 *a*) as having been drawn up for this particular ship's compass, then it is necessary to determine whether, when the ship's head is pointing on a magnetic course of 077°, there is any deviation of the compass, and allow for it if there is.

By reference to the deviation table or curve we find that for a magnetic course of 077° the deviation is 2° W.

Draw the line CA (Fig. 40) making an angle of 2° west of the magnetic meridian MA. (These angles need be drawn only approximately, provided that they are labelled with their values, as shown.) This line then represents the actual direction of the compass needle, known as the *compass meridian* when the vessel is steaming in the direction AB.

Consequently the *compass course* for the helmsman to steer is 077° + 2° = 079°.

It will have been noticed that the directions given in the deviation table or curve are for the "ship's head by compass". But, since the deviation is always reduced to a minimum by corrector magnets, and is seldom more than 3° either E. or W. on any course, there will be no appreciable error if the magnetic course of the ship is read instead of the compass course (as we have done above).

Never use the ship's true course for determination of deviation.

To avoid any possible mistake when stating a ship's compass course it is always given in compass notation, while the true course, as already stated, is given in three-figure notation.

Thus, the above compass course of 079° is always written N. 79° E., and a compass course of 193° is S. 13° W. A magnetic course is usually expressed in compass notation with the label (Mag.) to identify it.

Thus, a magnetic course of 288° is expressed as N. 72° W. (Mag.).

It is very often necessary to convert a compass course to a true course (for purposes of plotting on a chart) and in this case we simply reverse the proceeding and the corrections are made in the opposite order: compass course → deviation → magnetic course → variation → true course.

When correcting courses given in compass notation it is best, until practice has brought confidence, to convert the course into three-figure notation before the corrections are made. Label the corresponding three-figure readings with the letters (C) for compass and (M) for magnetic respectively, e.g. N. 16° W. = 344° (C). To be certain that no error is introduced it is advisable in all cases, until quite proficient, to draw a diagram.

EXAMPLE II. Convert a compass course of N. 72° W. to a true course, if variation is 8° W. and deviation is to be taken from the curve Fig. 39 a.

Draw CA (Fig. 41) to represent the compass meridian and make the angle $CAB = 72°$. Then AB represents the ship's compass course N. 72° W.

A compass course of N. 72° W. corresponds, in three-figure notation, to 360° − 72° = 288° (C).

For a compass course of 288° C (by reference to the deviation curve) the deviation is 1° E. The compass meridian is therefore *east* of the magnetic meridian by 1°. So that the magnetic meridian MA is 1° *west* of the compass meridian CA (as shown).

Therefore, we have, compass course = 288° (C)

deviation = 1° E. (+)

magnetic course = 289° (M)

The variation is 8° W., so that the magnetic meridian is *west* of the true meridian by 8°, i.e. the true meridian *TA* is 8° *east* of the magnetic meridian *MA* (as shown).

Thus, the magnetic course = 289° (M)
and   variation   =   8° W. (−)

            true course   = 281°

Therefore the true course corresponding to a compass course of N. 72° W. is, in this case, 281°.

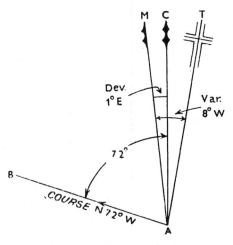

Fig. 41

Nearly every operation concerned with navigation at sea, when using a magnetic compass, involves the correction of a reading for deviation and variation errors.

It is therefore *most important* that no mistake is made in correcting these errors. There are several ways of checking the accuracy of the calculation, in addition to the above straightforward way, which should in any case be thoroughly mastered.

The Clockwise Rule.

This is an infallible check if correctly applied.

When the correction is made from Compass to Magnetic to True, i.e. from C to M to T, or in the correct order of the letters in the alphabet, then all *easterly* errors are added to the reading *clockwise* round the compass, and all westerly errors are anticlockwise.

EXAMPLE. What is the true course corresponding to a compass course of S. 21° E., if deviation is 2° E. and variation 8° W.?

A compass course of S. 21° E., in three-figure notation	$= 159°$ (C)
Deviation 2° E. (clockwise ↘)	$= \quad 2° +$
Magnetic course	$= 161°$ (M)
Variation 8° W. (anticlockwise ↙)	$= \quad 8° -$
True course	$= 153°$

For the reverse operation, i.e. from True to Magnetic to Compass, the initial letters may be taken to mean 'Take More Care!

In this case the easterly error is anticlockwise, and the westerly error is clockwise.

The Gyro Compass.

On most modern ships the "master" compass, by which all navigation is controlled, is a mechanically-operated gyroscopic instrument which does not depend, for its accuracy, upon the earth's magnetism; nor is it influenced by any local magnetism of the ship itself.

Consequently such considerations as variation and deviation do not arise, and the only error to which a gyro compass is subject is a slight discrepancy of 1° or 2° from the true reading. This error, if present at all, is consistent for all courses on which the ship may be heading and is termed "high" or "low" according as the compass reads high or low, e.g. true reading 146°; gyro reading 144°; gyro error 2° *low*.

Unless otherwise stated a gyro reading is assumed to be a true reading.

Nevertheless a knowledge, and understanding, of the use of a magnetic compass is very necessary, both in the navigation of small craft and as a safeguard should the mechanical machinery of a gyro compass break down or be damaged in action.

EXERCISE 7. Correct the following true courses to magnetic courses, using the variation shown.

No.	True course	Variation	No.	True course	Variation
1.	035°	10° E.	6.	022°	11° E.
2.	111°	4° W.	7.	216°	2° W.
3.	192°	5° W.	8.	152°	6° W.
4.	274°	11° E.	9.	306°	4° E.
5.	332°	4° E.	10.	358°	7° W.

EXERCISE 8. Correct the following magnetic courses to true courses, using the variation shown.

No.	Magnetic course	Vari- ation	No.	Magnetic course	Vari- ation
1.	N. 28° E. (Mag.)	4° E.	6.	N. 05° E. (Mag.)	12° W.
2.	S. 42° E. „	5° W.	7.	S. 28° E. „	4° E.
3.	S. 21° W. „	6° E.	8.	S. 89° W. „	10° W.
4.	N. 66° W. „	11° W.	9.	N. 88° W. „	8° W.
5.	N. 02° W. „	5° E.	10.	N. 05° W. „	12° E.

EXERCISE 9. Using the deviation curve Fig. 39 a, write down the deviations of the ship's compass for the following directions of the ship's head. (Answer to the nearest $\frac{1}{2}$°.)

No.	Ship's head by compass	Deviation	No.	Ship's head by compass	Deviation
1.	N. 45° E.		6.	N. 24° E.	
2.	S. 85° W.		7.	N. 71° W.	
3.	N. 15° W.		8.	S. 14° E.	
4.	N. 10° E.		9.	S. 52° E.	
5.	S. 75° E.		10.	N. 09° W.	

EXERCISE 10. Course correction from true to compass. Complete the following table using deviation curve Fig. 39 a.

No.	True course	Variation	Magnetic course	Deviation	Compass course
1.	205°	10° E.			
2.	139°	8$\frac{1}{2}$° E.			
3.	324°	7$\frac{1}{2}$° W.			
4.	055°	14° W.			
5.	159°	13° E.			
6.	214°	9° W.			
7.	350°	8$\frac{1}{2}$° E.			
8.	357°	7° W.			
9.	003°	3° E.			
10.	078°	13° W.			

EXERCISE 11. Course correction from compass to true. Complete the following table using deviation curve Fig. 39 a.

No.	Compass course	Deviation	Magnetic course	Variation	True course
1.	S. 50° E.			10° W.	
2.	S. 20° W.			12° E.	
3.	N. 40° W.			7° E.	
4.	N. 50° E.			8½° W.	
5.	S. 17° E.			10½° W.	
6.	S. 60° W.			6½° E.	
7.	N. 21° W.			9° W.	
8.	N. 08° W.			11° E.	
9.	S. 79° W.			14½° W.	
10.	N. 03° W.			3½° W.	

Visible Bearings.

The bearing of an object from an observer is the direction of the object relative to a meridian passing through the position of the observer.

If it is measured from the true meridian it is a *true* bearing, if measured from the magnetic meridian it is a *magnetic* bearing, and if measured from the compass meridian (i.e. the direction of the magnetic compass needle) it is a *compass* bearing.

A ship's compass is usually fitted with a special sighting arrangement, known as an azimuth mirror, for taking bearings of visible charted objects. A bearing, taken carefully, can be an accurate guide as to a ship's position when at sea.

If taken by magnetic compass, as a compass bearing, it must be corrected for deviation and variation of the ship's compass before it can be plotted on the chart as a true bearing.

In this connection there is one very important point to remember. The correction of a bearing for deviation must be made for the direction of the ship's head by compass (i.e. the compass course of the ship) and *not* for the bearing itself.

EXAMPLE I. In Fig. 42 a vessel is shown steaming on a true course of 277°. The compass bearing, at a certain time, of a light vessel V, just offshore, is S. 40° E. What is the true bearing of the light vessel, if the variation for that region is 11° W. and the deviation curve Fig. 39 a applies to the ship's compass?

It is first of all necessary to convert the ship's true course to a magnetic course so that we can determine, from the curve, the correct deviation to apply to the ship's compass.

The ship's true course = 277°
Variation = 11° W. + (clockwise)

Ship's magnetic course = 288° (M)
Deviation (for course 288° (M)) = 1° E. − (anticlockwise)

Therefore ship's compass course = 287° (C)

(Check this calculation by diagram.)

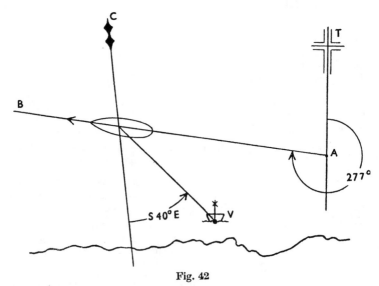

Fig. 42

The compass bearing of the light vessel S. 40° E., when

Converted into three-figure notation = 180° − 40°
= 140° (C)
Deviation (for ship's compass course 287° C) = 1° E. + (clockwise)

Magnetic bearing of light vessel = 141° (M)
Variation = 11° W. − (anticlockwise)

Therefore the true bearing of light vessel = 130°.

Note. Remember that compass bearings as such cannot be plotted on a chart. They must, before plotting, be corrected either to magnetic bearings (and plotted from the magnetic meridian on the compass roses) or to true bearings (and plotted from the true meridian).

EXAMPLE II. At 20 00 hr. a vessel is in position 49° 45′ N., 5° 00′ W. steaming at 10 knots on a compass course of N. 76° W., without any tidal drift. Using the practice chart and the deviation curve Fig. 39 *a*, where necessary, find (*a*) the ship's true course, (*b*) the true bearing of LIZARD HEAD LIGHT at 20 00 hr., (*c*) the compass bearing of LIZARD HEAD LIGHT at 20 00 hr., (*d*) the compass bearing of WOLF LIGHT at 22 30 hr.

(*a*) A compass course of N. 76° W.   = 360° − 76°

                                         = 284° (C)

     Deviation (for compass course 284° C) =   1° E. + (clockwise)

     Ship's magnetic course   = 285° (M)
     Variation   = 13° W. − (anticlockwise)

     Therefore the ship's true course   = 272°

(*b*) From the chart we find that the true bearing of LIZARD HEAD LIGHT from the ship's position at 20 00 hr. is 328°.

(*c*) The true bearing of LIZARD HEAD LIGHT = 328°
     Variation   = 13° W. +

                                        (clockwise)

     Magnetic bearing of LIZARD HEAD LIGHT = 341° (M)
     Deviation (for ship's compass course 284° C) = 1° E . −

                                          (anticlockwise)

     Therefore compass bearing of LIZARD
            HEAD LIGHT   = 340° (C)
                                      = N. 20° W.

(*d*) By plotting the ship's D.R. position at 22 30 hr. and measuring by protractor or from the true rose we find the true bearing of

WOLF LIGHT   = 326°
Variation   = 13° W. + (clockwise)

Magnetic bearing of WOLF LIGHT   = 339° (M)
Deviation (for ship's compass course 284° C) = 1° E. − (anticlockwise)

Therefore compass bearing of WOLF LIGHT = 338° (C)
                                      = N. 22° W.

EXERCISE 12. Use the practice chart and deviation curve Fig. 39 *a* where necessary and assume throughout this exercise that there is no tidal drift.

1. At 08 00 hr. a ship, which is steaming at 12 knots on a compass course of S. 60° W., is 10′ distant from Eddystone Lt., the compass bearing of which is N. 46° E., from the ship. Find the latitude and longitude of the ship's D.R. position at 10 00 hr.

2. At 15 30 hr. a vessel was in position 49° 41′ N., 6° 00′ W., steaming on a compass course of N. 14½° E. at 15 knots. Find the compass bearings of Longships Lt. and Seven Stones Lt. vessel at 17 30 hr.

3. At 19 00 hr. a vessel was 15′ from Wolf Lt. and 18′ from Lizard Head Lt. She was steaming on a straight course so as to clear Eddystone Lt. by 8′ and to leave it on the port hand, using 20 knots. Find (a) the ship's latitude and longitude at 19 00 hr., (b) her compass course, (c) the time when the compass bearing of Eddystone Lt. from the ship was N. 40° W.

4. A vessel to the westward of Start Pt. is in latitude 50° 10′ N. at 19 20 hr. and Start Pt. Lt. is 12′ distant. Her compass course is S. 72° W., and her speed is 14 knots. In what longitude and at what time will she cross the latitude parallel of 49° 50′ N.?

5. At 21 12 hr. a ship is 15′ from the Longships Lt. and 12′ from Lizard Head Lt. and is steaming at 16 knots on a compass course of S. 70° E. Find (a) the magnetic bearing and distance of the Wolf Lt. from her position at 21 12 hr., (b) the time when Lizard Head Lt. will be abeam to port.

6. A vessel is in a position 5′ from the Wolf Lt. so that this light and Longships Lt. are in line. Find (a) her compass course to steer to a position 20′ true south of Eddystone Lt., (b) the compass course to return along the same rhumb track.

7. If a vessel steams in a clockwise direction in a circle of radius 6′ whose centre is in position 49° 35′ N., 6° 30′ W., what will be the greatest and least compass bearings of Bishop Rock Lt.?

8. If a vessel steams for $2\frac{1}{2}$ hr. at 16 knots on a compass course east, from a position 49° 30′ N., 5° 40′ W., by how many minutes will she alter her (a) latitude, (b) longitude?

ESTIMATED POSITION

Of the four methods used for determining a ship's position when at sea (p. 9) we have, so far, considered only the first, dead-reckoning position. The important difference between this and the *estimated* position is that the latter does make the necessary allowance for the effects of ocean currents, tidal streams and leeway.

The waters of the seas and oceans are rarely stationary. Currents flow in them and these, in open water, are fairly constant in *set* (direction) and *rate* (speed).

In tidal waters, closer in shore, these movements are known as tidal streams and are mainly dependent upon the state of the tide, and vary considerably between high and low water. Tide is the movement of the water in an up and down direction; it is incorrect to refer to the horizontal flow of water as "tide". These movements are tidal streams. The set of a current or tidal stream is the direction in which it is moving and the rate of a current or tidal stream is its speed in knots.

The set is nearly always expressed as a true direction, e.g. 148°.

Scalar and Vector Quantities.

If a vessel is steaming at a speed of, say, 12 knots, and if this speed is represented on a scale of 1 in. = 1 knot, then any line 12 in. in length will represent the speed of the ship. Such a line is a *scalar* quantity, because it is drawn to scale.

This line does not take into account one important feature of the ship's movement. It does not give any indication of the direction of movement. Suppose, for example, that the vessel is steaming on a true course of 055°.

If, from any convenient point on a line drawn to represent the true meridian, a line is drawn at an angle of 055° clockwise from this meridian, then this line, if made 12 in. long, will represent both the speed *and* direction of the ship. Such a line is called a *vector*.

When a ship is steaming in a mass of water which is itself in motion, then the vessel, *in addition* to its own speed and direction, is carried with the current in the same direction and at the same speed as the current.

The ship is said to be "set" in the flow of the current by the amount known as the *drift*. This drift is measured in nautical miles.

Thus a current whose rate is 3 knots and whose set is 045° would, in 2 hr., cause the vessel to drift 6 n.m. in a direction true north-east of her D.R. position.

EXAMPLE I. Suppose that a ship, at 12 00 hr., was 8′ true south of START POINT LIGHT, and was steaming at 12 knots on a true course of 270° (Fig. 43). In this region the tidal stream is setting (say) 062° at 3 knots. What is the ship's estimated position at 14 00 hr.?

Let the point *A* denote the ship's position, 8′ true south of START POINT LIGHT at 12 00 hr. (Scale 1 in. = 8 n.m.)

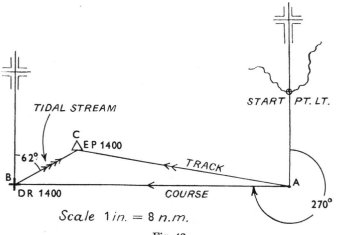

Fig. 43

Between 12 00 hr. and 14 00 hr., assuming that there were no tide, the ship would steam 24 n.m. in a direction 270° from the true meridian and her D.R. position would then be the point *B*.

This is labelled +D.R. 14 00.

But, during these two hours, the tidal stream between *A* and *B* would have caused the ship to drift. So that, in two hours, the drift and set of the vessel would be 6 n.m. in a direction 062°. This would carry the ship from the point *B* to the point *C*. The point *C*, therefore, is the ship's estimated position at 14 00 hr., and it is labelled on the chart with a small triangle followed by the time at which the position was established, e.g. △ E.P. 14 00. A vector of a tidal stream or ocean current is usually labelled with four arrows.

The line *AC* denotes the actual path of the vessel between 12 00 hr. and 14 00 hr., and is therefore a vector of the ship's *track*, i.e. her movement relative to sea bottom. It is usually labelled with double arrows. It must be clearly understood that although the ship's track is along *AC* (which by measurement is 279°) her head was kept throughout on a course of 270°, and the ship was drifting, all the time, to starboard. So that, in a tidal stream or ocean current, a vessel never travels in the same direction as her fore and aft line, unless the stream or current is setting dead ahead or dead astern.

The importance of this will be appreciated in the following example:

EXAMPLE II. A vessel whose course is represented by *CO* (Fig. 44) is actually making good a track *TR*. What will be her position when the charted light *L* is abeam to port?

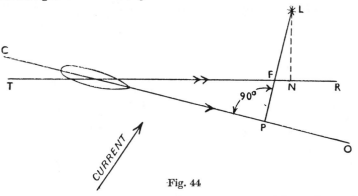

Fig. 44

The light *L* will be abeam when its direction is at right angles to the ship's fore and aft line.

If we draw *LP* perpendicular to *CO* we see that this line cuts the track line *TR* at *F*.

The point *F*, therefore, is the position of the ship when the light *L* is abeam to port. Notice particularly that it is *not* the point *N*.

Speed in a Tidal Stream.

When a ship is steaming in a tidal stream, or in an ocean current, her actual speed made good (i.e. her speed relative to sea bottom) is different from her engine speed.

EXAMPLE. A ship is steaming on a true course of 110° at 12 knots and a tidal stream is setting 351° at a rate of 4 knots. What is the ship's actual speed made good?

Using a suitable scale (say, 1 in. = 4 knots) draw a line *AB*, 3 in. in length, making an angle of 110° with the true meridian.

AB is then a vector of the ship's true course (110°) and her speed (12 knots) (Fig. 45).

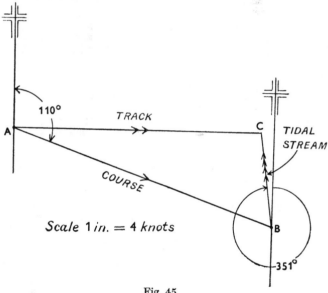

Fig. 45

At *B* plot the line *BC*, a vector of the rate (4 knots) and set (351°) of the tidal stream.

Join *AC*. Then the line *AC* is a vector of the ship's track.

By measurement, $AC = 2.7$ in., so that the ship's actual speed made good is $4 \times 2.7 = 10.8$ knots.

Note. When chart plotting a ship's estimated position in a tidal stream, the total allowance for drift and set is made at the end of the run, after plotting the ship's D.R. position, even though the ship may alter course on the journey.

EXERCISE 13. Where questions are based upon the practice chart use the variation as given on the chart. Use the deviation curve Fig. 39 *a* where necessary.

1. A ship is steaming on a true course of 255° at a speed of 12 knots. There is a tidal stream setting 187° at 2½ knots. Find (*a*) the ship's true track, (*b*) the speed made good along this track.

2. A vessel is steaming on a true course of 206° at 11 knots and a tidal stream is setting 330° at 2 knots. Find (*a*) the ship's true track, (*b*) the distance she would steam in 3 hr.

3. At 13 00 hr. a ship is in position 49° 30′ N., 6° 35′ W., steaming at 12 knots on a true course of 092°. At 15 30 hr. course is altered to 084°. If the tidal stream throughout is setting 004° at 3 knots, what is the ship's estimated position at 17 00 hr.?

4. At 14 00 hr. a vessel is in position 49° 40′ N., 6° 30′ W., steaming at 12 knots on a compass course of N. 80° E. At 16 00 hr. course is altered to S. 70° E. and at 17 30 hr. course is again altered to S. 85° E. If the tidal stream throughout is setting 107° at 2 knots, what is the ship's estimated position at 19 00 hr.?

5. A vessel is in position 50° 03′ N., 3° 35′ W. at 09 00 hr. and steaming at 10 knots on a compass course of S. 80° W. At 10 30 hr. course is altered to S. 10° W. and at 11 54 hr. she increases speed to 12 knots and shapes a new course of S. 60° W. There is a tidal stream setting 027° throughout at 3 knots. Find the latitude and longitude of the ship's estimated position at noon.

6. A ship's true course is 300° and her speed 11 knots. If a tidal stream is setting 240° at 3 knots and the variation is 10° W., find (*a*) the ship's magnetic track, (*b*) the speed made good along this magnetic track.

7. A vessel is in position 10 n.m. true north-west of Longships Lt. at 22 15 hr. She is steaming on a compass course of S. 04½° W. at 16 knots. At 23 45 hr. her course is altered to S. 89½° E. and her speed reduced to 12 knots. If a tidal stream is setting throughout 212° at 3 knots, find (*a*) the true track made good between 22 15 hr. and 23 45 hr., (*b*) the estimated position at 04 45 hr.

8. At noon a ship is 8′ true south-east of Bishop Rock Lt. She is steaming on a compass course of N. 85° E. at 10 knots. A tidal stream is setting 137° at 3 knots. Find (*a*) the ship's true track, (*b*) the speed made good along this track, (*c*) the time when Lizard Head Lt. is abeam to port.

9. A vessel is 5′ true south of Eddystone Lt. at 18 00 hr., and is steaming at 10 knots on a compass course S. 69½° W. Find (*a*) the nearest distance to starboard of Lizard Head Lt. as she proceeds on her course, (*b*) the time when she will be nearest to it, if, throughout, a tidal stream is setting 305° at 3 knots.

10. The compass course of a vessel is S. 16° E. and her engine speed is 10 knots. Her compass track is known to be S. 24° E. and her actual speed made good is 11 knots. If the local variation is 9° E., what is the rate and set of the tidal stream?

Shaping Course to make Good a Required Track, allowing for a Tidal Stream.

This is a most important application of the foregoing principles, because when steaming a straight course from one position to another in a tidal stream it is the true track of a ship that is represented by the rhumb line joining those two positions on a chart, and *not* the true course. So that, if a navigator wishes to travel any particular track he must shape such a course as will make allowance for the set and rate of the tidal stream.

EXAMPLE. Suppose that a vessel is in the position A (Fig. 46) and the navigator wishes to shape a course to clear the rock B by 2 n.m. and to leave it on his port hand. The ship's engine speed is 10 knots and the tidal stream is known to be setting 320° at 2 knots.

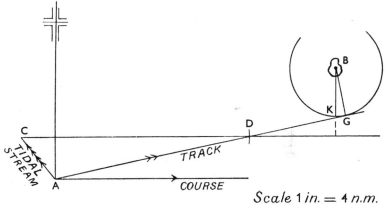

Scale 1 *in.* = 4 *n.m.*

Fig. 46

First of all select a suitable scale, say 1 in.=4 n.m. Then with the rock B as centre, a clearing circle of 2 n.m. radius is drawn and from A a tangent is then drawn to touch the circle at G. The line AG then represents the required track. From A draw AC, a vector of the set and rate of the tidal stream. With centre C and radius 2·5 in. (representing the ship's engine speed per hour) describe an arc cutting the track line AG at D. Join CD. Then CD represents the true course to be steered. This should be transferred by parallels through A, since it is from A that the course has to be set. By measurements this true course is 089°. Notice, as before mentioned, that the rock B is abeam to port when the ship has reached the point K on the track and not the point G.

In practice, when using a magnetic compass, the navigator would need to correct the above true course of 089° to a compass course before shaping his actual course.

EXERCISE 14. Work questions 1–5 on drawing paper, to a suitable scale, and questions 6–10 on the practice chart, using deviation curve Fig. 39 a where necessary.

1. What is the true course for a ship to steer at 12 knots so as to make good a track of 075° if the tidal stream is setting 310° at 3 knots?

2. A vessel is required to make good a track of 205° with a tidal stream setting 115° at 3½ knots. If the vessel is to use a speed of 13½ knots, find (a) the true course to steer, (b) the speed made good along the track.

3. (a) What true course should be shaped for a ship steaming at 10 knots to make good a track of 285° when the tidal stream is setting true south at 2½ knots? (b) What is the speed made good along this track?

4. A navigator wishes to make good a speed of 12 knots along a track of 132° in spite of a current setting 030° at 3 knots. Find (a) the true course he should shape, (b) the speed he should use.

5. A river flowing true east is 2 n.m. wide. A motor boat, using a speed of 6 knots, plies across the river from a point on the south bank to a point on the north bank, 2 n.m. up stream. If the river flows at 1½ knots, find (a) the true course to steer and the time of passage from the south bank, (b) the true course to steer and the time of passage when returning. Answer to the nearest minute.

6. A vessel, at noon, is in position 49° 40′ N., 5° 20′ W., and the navigator wishes to shape a course to pass 5′ true east of Eddystone Lt. If the tidal stream is setting magnetic north at 3 knots and the speed of the ship is 10 knots, find (a) the true course to steer, (b) the compass course to steer, (c) the speed made good, (d) the time when Eddystone Lt. is abeam.

7. A ship is in position 49° 30′ N., 4° 10′ W., at 13 00 hr. Course is to be shaped to clear Bishop Rock Lt. by 7′ on the starboard hand. The tidal stream is setting 027° at 3 knots. The navigator wishes to make good 10 knots along the track. Find (a) the true course to steer, (b) the compass course, (c) the ship's steaming speed, (d) the time when Bishop Rock Lt. is abeam to starboard.

8. At 14 00 hr. a vessel is 8′ due south of Eddystone Lt. and steaming on a compass course of S. 72½° W. at 12 knots. (a) State the D.R. position at 17 00 hr. If, at 17 00 hr., the navigator finds himself to be 5′ due south of Lizard Head Lt., state (b) the set and drift of the vessel experienced since 14 00 hr., (c) the set and rate of the tidal stream. From his actual position at 17 00 hr. the navigator wishes to shape a course to pass 5′ due south of Bishop Rock Lt., allowing for the effect of the tidal stream just determined. Find (d) his compass course to steer, (e) the speed made good.

9. A vessel, in fog, is 6' true south-east of Lizard Head Lt. at 22 00 hr., and the navigator shapes course for Mewstone to make Plymouth Sound, at a speed of 10 knots. He makes no allowance for a tidal stream which is setting north-east (Mag.) at 2 knots. At what time and in what position will the ship run aground?

10. A vessel leaves Plymouth and at 10 15 hr. she is 11' true south of Mewstone. Course is then shaped for a rendezvous 12' true south of Wolf Lt. Allowance is made for a current setting 317° at 3 knots. Her steaming speed is 11 knots. Find (a) the compass course to steer and the time of arrival at the rendezvous, (b) the compass course to return and the time of arrival at position 11' true south of Mewstone, if she sets out to return at 18 00 hr.

FIXES

We come now to the third and most important of the methods for finding a ship's position in coastal waters.

There are many types of fix, but all make use of charted visible objects, and the position lines which can be drawn from them.

A fix should always be labelled with a small circle and dot with the time at which it was taken, e.g. ⊙ Fix 14 12.

Bearing and Distance.

A compass bearing of any visible charted object and its distance from the observer constitute a fix by "bearing and distance". When taken by magnetic compass the bearing must be corrected for deviation and variation (remembering always that the deviation error is read for the ship's compass heading and *not* for the bearing). This true bearing is then laid off, on the chart, as a position line, from the object, by parallels through the rose, or by ruler and protractor. The distance along this position line, from the object, fixes the ship's position. The possibility of error in estimating the distance from the object makes this fix less reliable.

Transit and Distance.

This is very similar to the method given above except that in this case two charted objects are observed. When they are directly in line, as viewed from the ship, they are said to be "in transit", and if the two objects are *A* and *B*, this is usually denoted by the symbol $A \phi B$. There is no need to take any observation other than the time of the transit, and the distance from the nearest object, since the position line afforded by the transit is laid down directly on the chart (see Fig. 47).

A and *B* are the objects in transit, *ABC* is the position line and *F* is the fix, if the length *BF* represents the ship's distance from *B*.

Fig. 47

Cross Bearings.

If compass bearings of two different charted objects *A* and *B* are taken, immediately after each other, the true bearings (after correction) of these two objects, when plotted as position lines, will intersect and the point of intersection, *F*, is the fix (Fig. 48).

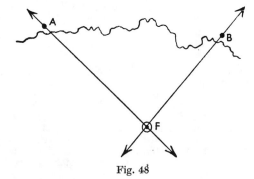

Fig. 48

It must be remembered, as previously stated (p. 9), that, for the fix to be reliable, the angle of cut of the position lines should be not less than 30°. When taking cross bearings the readings should be taken as quickly as possible, consistent with accuracy, and the bearing which is changing more rapidly should be taken last.

For example, if one charted object is on the starboard beam and the other on the port bow, it is the starboard bearing which is changing more quickly than the port bearing and is consequently taken after the port bearing.

The Cocked Hat.

As a check upon the accuracy of a cross bearing it is advisable when possible to take a bearing of a third object (keeping in mind the above rule of rapidity of change of bearing), and these three bearings, when corrected for deviation and variation, and plotted on the chart, will form a small triangle known as a *cocked hat*. If the readings had been taken with absolute accuracy all at the same time, the position lines would intersect at a point, so that if the cocked hat actually obtained is a large one the error may be due to (1) the bearings having been taken badly, (2) the bearings having been corrected wrongly for deviation and variation, (3) the objects having been wrongly identified. The readings should be made again so that the result is more in keeping with accuracy.

For safety, the fix in a cocked hat is always considered to be that corner of the triangle which places the ship nearest to any danger.

Transit and Bearing.

In this case also a third charted object is necessary in addition to the two in transit, so that a bearing can be read from the third object.

A fix by transit and compass bearing is recorded in this manner: $A \phi B$, N. 36° W., C.

EXERCISE 15. Plot the following fixes on the chart and state the latitude and longitude of the fix in each case. Use the curve Fig. 39 a for deviation.

No.	Time	Ship's compass course	Fix
1.	10 00	N. 50° E.	Wolf Lt. ϕ Longships Lt., 5′ from Wolf Lt.
2.	21 15	S. 35° E.	St Mary's Lt., 8′ distant, bears S. 80½° W.
3.	22 00	S. 40° W.	St Anthony Pt. Lt., bears N. 29° W.
			Lizard Head Lt., bears N. 89° W.
4.	23 15	E.	Wolf Lt., bears N. 23½° W.
			Lizard Head Lt., bears N. 70½° E.
5.	12 00	S.	Eddystone Lt. bears S. 63½° W., Mewstone 5′
6.	14 30	N. 38° E.	Hensbarrow Beacon ϕ Gribbin Head
			N. 85° W. Dodman Pt.
7.	19 30	N. 15° W.	Start Pt. Lt., bears S. 80° W.
			Berry Head Lt., bears N. 12° W.
8.	15 00	S. 40° W.	Eddystone Lt., bears S. 27° E.
			Rame Head, bears N. 76° E.
9.	11 45	S. 10° E.	Longships Lt., bears S. 31° E.
			Wolf Lt., bears S. 14° W.
			Seven Stones Lt., bears S. 89° W.
10.	12 30	S. 41° W.	Trevose Head Lt., bears S. 26° W.
			Pentire Pt., bears S.
			Brown Willy, bears S. 47° E.

The Running Fix with no Tidal Stream.

This is a useful type of fix, as it enables a navigator to establish his position when only one charted object is visible, or when two charted objects are not visible at the same time. It consists of taking two compass bearings of the same object, or of two different objects, with a "run" between the times of observation.

EXAMPLE. Suppose that a vessel was in the D.R. position shown (Fig. 49) at 09 48 hr. and was steaming at 10 knots on the true course indicated. At 10 00 hr. a bearing of A was taken by compass and, after

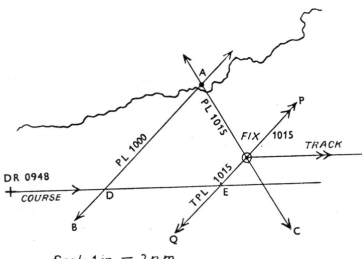

Scale 1 *in.* = 2 *n.m.*

Fig. 49

correction, the true bearing was plotted giving the position line AB (labelled P.L. 10 00 and indicated by reversed arrows). At 10 15 hr. a second compass bearing of A, when corrected, gave the position line AC (labelled P.L. 10 15). These, since they do not intersect, do not provide a fix as they stand. But during the interval (15 min.), between taking the two bearings, the ship has travelled a distance of $2\frac{1}{2}$ n.m. If we mark off this distance to scale ($1\frac{1}{4}$ in.) from D, the point where the first position line AB cuts the course, we reach the point E. At E draw another line PQ parallel to AB. This is called a "transferred position line" and is indicated with double reversed arrows, as shown, and labelled T.P.L. 10 15, showing that it was a position line at 10 15 hr.

Now we have two position lines upon which the ship is situated *at the same time*, so that the point of intersection of the P.L. 10 15 and T.P.L. 10 15 is the fix, and is labelled accordingly ⊙ Fix 10 15.

By drawing, through this fix, a line parallel to the course, we have the ship's track.

The Running Fix allowing for a Tidal Stream.

Had there been a tidal stream running in the above example we should have had to allow for it for the 15 min. interval between the taking of the bearings.

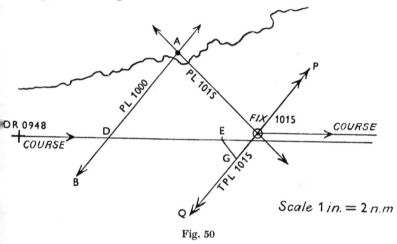

Fig. 50

If we assume that a stream is setting 135° at 2 knots, then the drift of the ship in 15 min. would be ½ n.m. and the set would be 135°, which would carry her from the point E to the point G (Fig. 50). It is through the point G, therefore, that the transferred position line PQ is drawn in this case.

Notice here, that the parallel line drawn through the fix is *not* the ship's track. It still only represents her true course. Her track would be found, from the fix, by allowance for the run of the tidal stream, as already done in previous exercises.

If the ship's track were known with certainty, and also her speed made good along it, then these could be plotted directly, as the course has been in Fig. 49, since the allowance for the run of the tidal stream would have been made already in establishing the ship's track.

A method similar to the above is used in cases where bearings are taken of two different objects instead of the same object.

Red and Green Bearings (Relative Bearings).

There are several special and useful cases of the running fix, where measurements of the bearings are made in a different way.

The bearings of objects are often taken relative to the ship's fore and aft line, and have no reference to any meridian. These are known as relative bearings.

By an observer, in a ship, the port side is often referred to as the "red" side, and the starboard side as the "green" side.

If we measure bearings from dead ahead (0°) on the ship's fore and aft line to dead astern (180°), we can have any readings between 0° and 180° on the port side (red) or on the starboard side (green). Reference to Fig. 51 will show that the bearing referred to as "port bow" may also be called Red 45°, while "starboard quarter" is Green 135°.

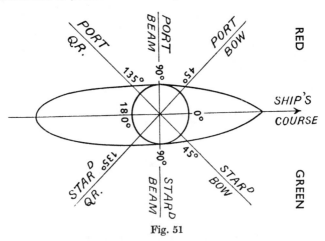

Fig. 51

Any red or green bearing may be converted into a compass bearing and then to a true bearing.

EXAMPLE. Suppose that a ship is steaming on a compass course of N. 58° E. and that an object A bears Green 35° (Fig. 52). Then, obviously, the compass bearing of this object would be

$$35° + N. 58° E. = N. 93° E., \quad \text{i.e.} \quad S. 87° E.$$

If the object B bears Red 90°, then the compass bearing of B from the ship is the reflex angle $COB = 360° - $ angle COB

$$= 360° - (90° - 58°)$$
$$= 360° - 32°$$
$$= 328°$$

i.e. N. 32° W.

These bearings may be corrected to true bearings in the usual way, by allowing for deviation and variation of the ship's magnetic compass.

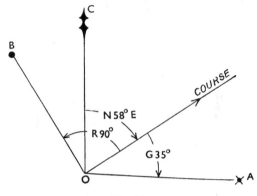

Fig. 52

EXERCISE 16. Use deviation curve Fig. 39 *a* where necessary.

1. When steaming on a true track of 120° to the southward of Bishop Rock Lt., a navigator found the bearing of the light at 10 21 hr. to be Red 45°. At 10 41 hr. the reading was Red 90°. If the speed of the ship was 18 knots, what was the fix at 10 41 hr.?

2. Steaming true north, with the Wolf Lt. to starboard, an observer, at 14 10 hr., read the bearing of Wolf Lt. as Green 44°. At 14 30 hr. the bearing was Green 97°. What was the fix at 14 30 hr., if the ship's speed was 15 knots?

3. From a ship, steaming up channel at 16 knots, the Lizard Head Lt. was seen to bear Red 65° at 19 20 hr., and Red 130° at 19 50 hr. The ship was steering a compass course of N. 70° E. Find the fix at 19 50 hr., assuming that there was no tidal stream.

4. A vessel was steaming on a compass course of S. 50° W. at 12 knots, and at 21 00 hr. the bearing of Eddystone Lt. was Green 40°. At 21 30 hr. the bearing of the same light was Green 79°. What was the ship's D.R. position at 22 30 hr.?

5. A ship was steaming at 15 knots on a compass course of N. 30° E. and at 22 15 hr. the navigator observed the bearing of Wolf Lt. to be N. 69° E. At 23 15 hr. the bearing of Longships Lt. was S. 54° E. What was the fix at 23 15 hr., if there were no tidal stream?

6. On a compass course N. 83° W. and a speed of 10 knots, an observer took a compass bearing of Eddystone Lt. at noon, which read N. 34° W. At 13 00 hr. the same light bore N. 46° E. What was the fix at 13 00 hr., if the tidal stream was setting 189° at 3 knots?

7. At 11 30 hr. a ship was in D.R. position 49° 50′ N., 4° 45′ W., steaming on a compass course of N. 78° W. at 15 knots. At 12 22 hr. the bearing of Lizard Head Lt. was N. 27° W. and at 13 02 hr. the bearing of the same light was N. 52° E. If the tidal stream was setting magnetic south at 3 knots, what was the ship's estimated position at 14 22 hr.?

8. At 14 00 hr. a vessel was steaming on a course of S. 89° W. and Start Pt. Lt. was on her starboard quarter. Her speed was 12 knots and a 4 knot tidal stream was setting 329°. The bearing of Eddystone Lt. at 15 00 hr. was found to be N. 38° W. Fix the ship's actual position at 14 00 hr.

9. A navigator in a ship steaming a course of N. 84° W., to the south-westwards of Wolf Lt., wishes to check the current in this region. At 21 18 hr. he sees Wolf Lt. and Longships Lt. to be in transit. His distance from Wolf Lt. is 6 n.m. At 23 18 hr. Bishop Rock Lt. is abeam to starboard and the bearing of St Mary's Lt. is Green 127°. If the ship's engine speed is 9 knots, what is the set and rate of the current?

10. A navigator in a ship steaming on a course of N. 45° E. takes bearings, at the same time, of St Anthony Pt. Lt. and Dodman Pt. to fix his position. These are N. 57° W. and N. 18° E. respectively. When plotting these on the chart he omits to correct them for deviation and variation. How far and in what compass direction is his true position from his false position?

THE SEXTANT

The sextant is a portable optical instrument used for the measurement of angles between distant objects. In open ocean, with no charted objects within his range of vision, the navigator has to depend upon the measurement of angular distances of the sun and stars above the horizon, to determine the ship's "observed position".

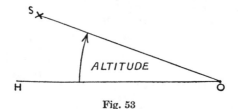

Fig. 53

These angular distances, or altitudes as they are called, can be determined with accuracy by means of the sextant. If *O* (Fig. 53) represents an observer, and *OH* a horizontal line from his eye to the distant horizon, then the altitude of the sun or stars *S*, above the horizon, is the angle *SOH*.

In Fig. 54, *AB* represents a ray of light falling upon a plane mirror surface at *B* and being reflected along the path *BC*. The line *BD*, drawn perpendicular to the mirror, is called a "normal".

The angle "*i*", which is the angle between the incident ray *AB* and the normal, and the angle "*r*", which is the angle between the normal and the reflected ray, are called the angles of *incidence* and *reflection* respectively.

Whenever a ray of light is reflected from a plane surface the angle of incidence is equal to the angle of reflection.

The sextant carries two mirrors. The first of these is known as the *horizon glass*, and the bottom half of it is silvered and the top half is a plain glass window for direct vision.

The second mirror, known as the *index glass*, is completely silvered.

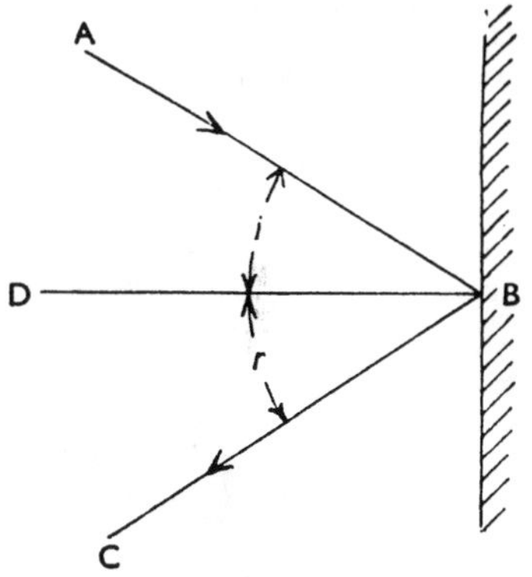

The observer sees the distant sea horizon by direct vision through the unsilvered half of the horizon glass *H* (Fig. 55).

Fig. 54

He rotates the index glass *I* until he sees the star *S*, whose ray of light has travelled along the path *SIHO* after reflection in both mirrors. It is then found that the altitude of the star, i.e. the angle *SOA*, is exactly double the angle of inclination of the two mirrors, or, which is the same thing, double the angle between their normals, i.e. the angle *SOA* = 2 × the angle *INH*.

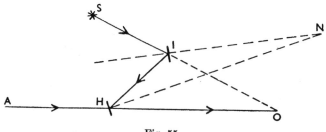

Fig. 55

The angle of inclination of the two mirrors is read on a graduated scale, known as the *arc*, of the sextant, and the graduations are made in *half* degrees but are marked as *whole* degrees. In this way the angle of inclination of the mirrors reads double its value and records the actual altitude of the star.

The following is a brief description of the working parts of a sextant as illustrated in Fig. 56.

A is the graduated arc of the instrument. The centre of the circle, of which this arc is a part, is also the dead centre of the pivot of the index glass *I*. The latter is rotated by means of the index bar *B* to which it is rigidly attached so that its plane is always exactly perpendicular to the

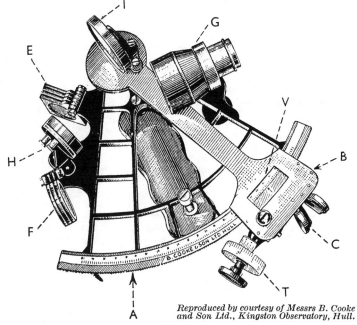

Reproduced by courtesy of Messrs B. Cooke and Son Ltd., Kingston Observatory, Hull.

Fig. 56

plane of the arc. The index bar *B* can be clamped, or moved in any position on to the arc itself by means of the clamping-release device *C* and further fine adjustments of measurement can be made by the tangent screw *T*. *H* is the partly silvered horizon glass. The letters *E* and *F* represent coloured glass shades for protecting the eye when observing the sun. A collar on the instrument allows of the fitting of a suitable telescope *G* according to the type of observation being made. The angle recorded on the arc is read by means of the vernier *V*.

Note. When practising with the sextant, angles should not be measured between objects within close range, because an error, due to "sextant parallax", will then cause unreliable and inaccurate readings.

Use of the Sextant in Fixing.

In addition to its use for purposes of finding a ship's observed position when at sea, from observations of heavenly bodies, the sextant is a most useful instrument for the determination of ordinary fixes, by the readings obtained from charted terrestrial objects.

EXAMPLE I. *A sextant fix with two charted objects.*

If a navigator reads the sextant angle between two charted objects *A* and *B*, which are both visible at the same time from the same position, and finds it to be, say, 50°, this observation does not, by itself, constitute a fix.

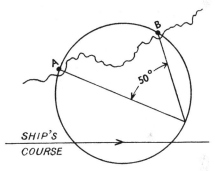

Fig. 57

Since all angles in a segment of a circle are equal, then the fix might be anywhere on the seaward arc of the circle as drawn through *A* and *B* (Fig. 57). It would be a fix when combined with either (*a*) the distance of the ship from *A* or *B*, or (*b*) the true bearing of either *A* or *B* from the ship.

EXAMPLE II. *A sextant fix with three charted objects.*

Two sextant angles, read at the same time, between three charted objects do provide an accurate fix, if care is taken to select them so that they do not, together with the ship's position, lie approximately on the circumference of the same circle.

In Fig. 58 the two sextant angles are, say, 58° between *A* and *B*, and 54° between *B* and *C*. (Such a reading is usually written *A* 58° (S) *B* 54° (S) *C*, where "S" denotes a sextant reading.)

In this case the two arcs intersect at *F*, and *F* is consequently the required fix.

Having taken the required sextant angles, the easiest way to fix the ship's position on the chart is to use tracing paper.

From any convenient point *F* on the paper draw a line *FB* (Fig. 59). To the right of *B* lay off the line *FA* at an angle of 58° and to the left of *B* the line *FC* at an angle of 54°. Always letter the lines with the objects to which they refer.

Place the tracing paper on the chart and adjust its position until each line passes through its respective charted object. Prick through, on to the chart, the position of *F*, the required fix.

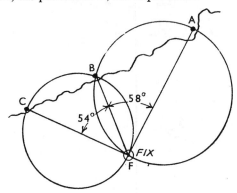

Fig. 58

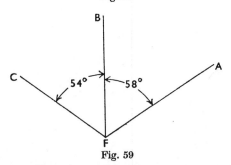

Fig. 59

EXERCISE 17. Use tracing paper for this exercise and plot, on the chart, the following sextant fixes, giving the latitude and longitude of the fix.

1. Wolf Lt. 29° S. Longships Lt. 116° S. Lizard Head Lt.
2. St Mary's Lt. φ Bishop Rock Lt. 46½° S. Seven Stones ⚓.
3. Gp. Fl. Cape Cornwall 27° S. Longships Lt. 28° S. Wolf Lt.
4. Dodman Pt. 48° S. Gribbin Head 132° S. Eddystone Lt.
5. Tintagel Head 30° S. Pentire Pt. 30° S. Trevose Head Lt.
6. Towan Head 48° S. St Agnes Head 39° S. Godrevy I. Lt.

INCLINATION AND DEFLECTION

When a ship is observed, from a distance, the course she is steering is not at once determinable. It is generally much easier to estimate her *inclination*. This is the angle at which she is crossing the line of sight. It is measured from the extended line of sight to the ship's bow, from 0° to 180°, and is named "right" or "left" according as the ship is crossing to right or to left of the line of sight.

Example I. A ship at *A* sights an enemy ship at *B* (Fig. 60) bearing Green 53° and inclination 106° right. The diagram will explain how this is interpreted.

When the speed of the enemy ship is known, as well as her inclination, we may, by simple scale drawing, express her speed as the two components of a right-angled triangle.

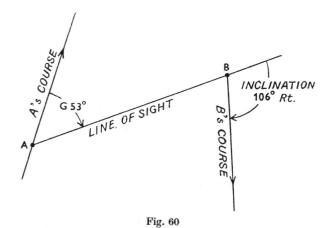

Fig. 60

Example II. The inclination of an enemy ship is 110° right, and her speed is 10 knots.

By drawing the right-angled triangle *BCD* to scale (say 1 in. = 4 knots), as shown in Fig. 61, this speed and direction may be "resolved" into two components *DC* and *BD*.

By measurement we find *DC* = 2·35 in. = 9·4 knots and *BD* = 0·85 in. = 3·4 knots.

The speed, at right angles to the line of sight, represented by *DC* is called the *deflection*. This also is expressed as right or left of the line of sight, and in this case the deflection is 9·4 knots right.

The speed *BD*, along the line of sight, is known as the *range rate* and is said to be *closing* when the enemy ship is approaching, and *opening* when she is receding.

In the above case the range rate is 3·4 knots closing.

In practice, for purposes of gun ranging, the range rate is converted from knots into *yards per minute*, assuming that one nautical mile is equal to 2000 yards.

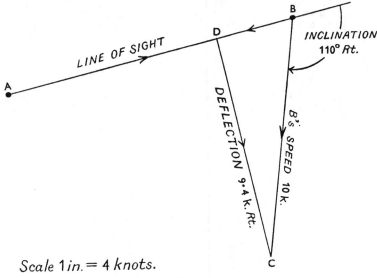

Scale 1 in. = 4 knots.

Fig. 61

So that the above range rate becomes:

$$3\text{·}4 \text{ n.m. in } 1 \text{ hr.}$$

$$=\frac{3\text{·}4 \times 2000}{60} \text{ yd. in } 1 \text{ min.}$$

$$=113 \text{ yards per minute, closing.}$$

It more often happens that a ship's deflection is known and the range rate also can be accurately determined by range-finding instruments, so that her inclination and actual speed may be easily calculated.

EXAMPLE III. An enemy ship shows deflection 8 knots left and the range rate is 560 yd. per min. opening. What is the ship's inclination and speed?

First convert the range rate from yards per min. into knots, i.e. range rate $= \dfrac{560 \times 60}{2000} = 16 \cdot 8$ knots, opening. Draw any convenient line AA' to represent the line of sight, and select any point B on it as the enemy ship's position (Fig. 62).

Using a suitable scale, 1 in. $= 5$ knots, measure a distance BC (by diagonal scale) of $3 \cdot 36$ in., to represent $16 \cdot 8$ knots range rate. Since this range rate is opening it is measured in the direction of the line of sight, away from the observer.

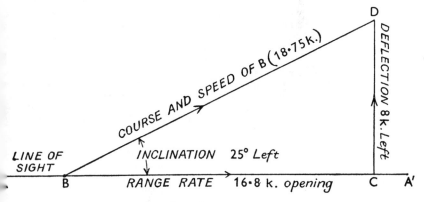

Scale 1 in. = 5 knots.

Fig. 62

At C draw CD at right angles to, and to the left of AA', so that CD is $1 \cdot 6$ in. $= 8$ knots deflection left. Join BD. Then the angle CBD is the inclination, which by measurement is found to be 25° left. The length of BD, to the above scale, represents the speed of the ship, i.e. $BD = 3 \cdot 75$ in., and the ship's speed is $18 \cdot 75$ knots.

EXERCISE 18. Use the chart to solve the first five questions and assume that 1 n.m. $= 2000$ yd. and that there is no tidal stream.

1. A vessel A, in position 49° 40′ N., 6° 00′ W., steaming on a true course 065° observes a ship B to bear Green 50° at a range of 20,000 yd. From A, the inclination of B is 100° left. Find (a) the position of B, (b) B's true course, (c) the fore and aft line bearing and inclination of A from B.

2. At 11 00 hr. a ship A was in position 49° 45′ N., 4° 30′ W., steaming at 12 knots on a true course of 020°. At 11 20 hr. a ship B was seen to bear Green 110° at a range of 16,000 yd. with inclination 80° right. At 12 20 hr. B reports by wireless that she has been disabled and stopped, and that her speed up to then was 10 knots. What true course should A steer to join B and at what time should she arrive if she continues at her same speed?

3. At 16 00 hr. a destroyer is in position 50° 25′ N., 6° 20′ W., and a corvette is in 50° 10′ N., 6° 10′ W. The destroyer is steaming 12 knots on a true course of 095° and the corvette is steaming 10 knots on a true course of 050°. Find (a) the range and inclination of the destroyer from the corvette at 16 30 hr., (b) whether the corvette will cross the destroyer's track ahead or astern of her, and by what distance, (c) the time when the corvette crosses the destroyer's track.

4. At 18 30 hr. a vessel A is in position 49° 30′ N., 5° 30′ W., steaming at 12 knots on a true course of 020°, and a second vessel B is observed to bear Green 60°, range 30,000 yd. At 19 00 hr. the ship B still bears Green 60° and the range has reduced to 20,000 yd. Find (a) the true course and speed of B, (b) the time and position of collision if the bearing of B from A does not alter.

5. A cruiser is in position 49° 35′ N., 5° 00′ W. at 17 00 hr., steaming on a true course of 035° at 15 knots. A destroyer distant 30′, on a bearing Green 65° from the cruiser, reports her course as 000° and speed 12 knots. At 17 30 the destroyer reports sighting an enemy vessel bearing Green 40°, inclination 70° right, range 20,000 yd., steaming at an estimated speed of 10 knots. The cruiser alters course at 17 30 hr. to 102° and increases speed to 20 knots. Find (a) the range at 19 00 hr. and the relative bearing of the enemy from the cruiser, (b) the inclination of the enemy at 19 00 hr.

Solve the remaining five questions by drawing to a suitable scale on plain paper, and assume that there is no tidal stream.

6. Two ships A and B are steaming in the same direction on parallel courses. From A, the vessel B is observed to bear Green 73°, with inclination 73° left, range 8000 yd. at 12 30 hr. The speed of A is 10 knots and the speed of B is 12 knots. At 13 00 hr. the vessel B alters course by two points to starboard. Find the range and inclination of B from A at 13 30 hr.

7. A destroyer at 15 00 hr. is steaming true north at 12 knots and observes an enemy cruiser bearing Green 48°, with inclination 148° left, speed 10 knots. The range is 13 nautical miles. At 15 15 hr. she fires a 30-knot torpedo on a bearing Green 40°. By what distance, ahead or astern, will the torpedo miss the cruiser?

8. A cruiser, at 16 30 hr., was steaming on a true course of 120° at 12 knots and an enemy vessel was observed to bear Red 60° at 18,000 yd. range. The enemy's inclination was 70° right and her speed 10 knots. Find the enemy's range rate and deflection from the cruiser at (a) 16 30 hr., (b) 16 45 hr.

9. A cruiser was steaming on a true course of 110° at 12 knots, when, at noon, an enemy cruiser was sighted, at a range of 24,000 yd., on a bearing Red 80°, inclination 110° right and speed 18 knots. Find the range, range rate and deflection of the enemy at (a) 12 15 hr., (b) 12 30 hr.

10. At 11 30 hr. a submarine is stationary and submerged, and an enemy ship is observed bearing Red 102° at 14,000 yd. range. The enemy's speed is 10 knots and inclination 138° right. If the maximum range of the submarine's torpedoes is 10,000 yd., between what times must she fire her torpedoes to register a possible hit? The submarine remains stationary throughout.

NAVAL EDUCATIONAL TESTS

By kind permission of the Admiralty and the Controller of H.M. Stationery Office the following list of questions in elementary navigation is included for revision. The problems are selected from recent Admiralty test papers and, where called for, the practice chart provided should be used for their solution.

1. At 08 30 St Mary's Light bore 295°, Wolf Light bore 040°. Course of ship 085°. Speed 12 knots.

Plot the 08 30 position on the chart provided, and find the latitude and longitude of the ship's position at 12 00.

2. Your ship is steering 090° and an enemy ship is sighted bearing Red 65°. If the inclination of the enemy is 120° to the left, what is the enemy's course?

3. An aeroplane is flying at a height of 7500 feet, and the angle of sight of the aeroplane is 35°. Find, by drawing a figure to scale, the range of the aeroplane measured along the line of sight.

Use the scale 1 inch = 3000 feet, and express your answer in yards.

4. At 10 20 Lizard Head Light bore 265°, St Anthony Point Light bore 330°. Course 075°. Speed 15 knots.

Plot the 10 20 position on the chart provided, and find the latitude and longitude of the ship's position at 12 00.

5. Your ship is steering 270°, and an enemy ship is sighted bearing Green 75°. If the enemy is steering a course 245°, what is the inclination of the enemy?

6. An aeroplane is sighted at an angle of sight 30°, and the range is found by rangefinder to be 4500 yards. Find, by drawing to scale, the height (in feet) at which the aeroplane is flying.

Use the scale 1 inch = 1000 yards.

7. Wolf Light bears 083° and St Mary's Light bears 263°. Why cannot you fix your position by these bearings? At the same moment Longships Light bears 053°. Plot your position and give the latitude and longitude.

8. At 09 00 a ship A is in 49° 32' N., 6° W., steaming 090° at 16 knots; at the same time a ship B is in 49° 48' N., 6° W., steaming 100° at 16 knots. Plot the tracks of the two ships and mark their positions at 12 00.

What is the relative bearing, true bearing, inclination and range (in yards) of B from A at 12 00?

9. When steering 218°, a ship turns 4 points to starboard. What is the new course?

10. At 10 00 a ship A is in 49° 32' N., 5° W., steaming 270° at 17 knots; at the same time a ship B is in 49° 38' N., 5° W., steaming 260° at 17 knots. Plot the tracks of the two ships and mark their positions at 13 00.

What is the relative bearing, true bearing, inclination and range (in yards) of B from A at 13 00?

11. Longships Light bears 067° and St Mary's Light bears 247°. Why cannot your position be fixed by these bearings alone? At the same moment the Wolf Light bears 110°. Plot your position and give the latitude and longitude.

12. If a ship, on a course 183°, turns 4 points to port, what is her new course?

13. At 17 00 Berry Head Light bore 330°, Start Point Light bore 246°. Course 234°. Speed 16 knots.

Plot the 17 00 position on the chart, and find the latitude and longitude of the ship's D.R. position at 21 00.

14. A ship is steering a steady course at 12 knots. At 10 30 a light ship is observed bearing Green 22° and distant 13,000 yards. By means of a drawing to scale, taking 1 inch to represent 2000 yards, find at what time the light ship will be abeam, and what its distance will then be.

15. At 18 00 Start Point Light bore 256°, Berry Head Light bore 350°. Course 238°. Speed 15 knots.

Plot the 18 00 position on the chart, and find the latitude and longitude of the ship's D.R. position at 22 00.

16. A ship is steering a steady course at 16 knots. At 11 00 a light ship is observed bearing Red 37° and distant 10,000 yards. By means of a drawing to scale, taking 1 inch to represent 2000 yards, find at what time the light ship will be abeam, and what its distance will then be.

17. What is the bearing and distance of the Eddystone from Lizard Head?

18. Seven Stones light-vessel bears 309° and Longships Light bears 063°. Fix position on the chart and give the latitude and longitude.

19. Your own ship and an enemy ship are steaming in the same direction on parallel courses. If the enemy ship bears Red 70°, what is her inclination?

20. What is the bearing and distance of Wolf Light from Lizard Head?

21. Longships Light bears 063° and the Wolf Light bears 129°. Fix position on the chart and give the latitude and longitude.

22. Your own ship and an enemy ship are steaming in the same direction on parallel courses. If the enemy ship bears Green 65°, what is her inclination?

23. A cruiser steaming 150° observes an enemy craft bearing Red 60°, distant 9000 yards, and at the same time fires a 35-knot torpedo in a direction Red 35°. The enemy is steering 170° at 14 knots. After what interval of time does the torpedo cross the enemy's track? How far ahead or astern of the enemy does the torpedo pass?

24. A destroyer steaming 030° at 25 knots observes an enemy cruiser at 08 00 bearing Green 50°, distant 8000 yards. If the enemy is steaming 010° at 20 knots, what is her bearing and distance from the destroyer at 08 15, and at what time will the destroyer cross the cruiser's track?

25. A cruiser steaming 110° at 20 knots observes a liner at 12 00 bearing Red 120°, distant 9000 yards. If the liner is steaming 125° at 30 knots, what is her bearing and distance from the cruiser at 12 15, and at what time does the liner cross the cruiser's track?

26. At 08 00 a cruiser steaming 015° at 16 knots observes an enemy destroyer bearing Green 116°, range 8000 yards. At 08 15 the destroyer bears Green 76°, range 10,000 yards. Estimate the course and speed of the destroyer.

27. At 12 00 a cruiser steaming 105° at 15 knots observes a liner bearing Red 115°, range 7500 yards. At 12 20 the liner bears Red 86°, range 10,000 yards. Estimate the course and speed of the liner.

28. From a submarine steaming 010° an enemy ship bears Green 50°, distant 9000 yards. A 35-knot torpedo is fired in direction Green 70° and scores a hit on the enemy 9 minutes after firing. What is the course and speed of the enemy?

29. From a destroyer steaming 070° an enemy ship bears Red 80°, distant 8000 yards. A 35-knot torpedo is fired in direction Red 55° and scores a hit on the enemy 8 minutes after firing. What is the course and speed of the enemy?

30. A drifter with a speed of 8 knots sets out for a port 20 miles away and bearing 320°. There is a current of $3\frac{1}{2}$ knots setting 050°. Find

(*a*) What course the drifter should steer.

(*b*) The time taken to reach the port.

31. (*a*) From a ship steering 050° the inclination of a target ship bearing Red 80° was observed to be 110° right. What was the true course of the target?

(*b*) The true bearing of a point of land was 167° and its compass bearing was S. 3° W. The variation was 14° W. Find the deviation of the compass.

32. At 10 00 a steamer bore 120° from a warship and was distant 15 miles. Course and speed of steamer 250°, 15 knots. Course and speed of warship 170°, 12 knots. Find

(*a*) The time when the distance between the two ships has decreased to 7 miles.

(*b*) The least distance between the two ships.

(*c*) The time when the distance between the two ships is again 7 miles.

33. *A* and *B* are two lights 16 miles apart on opposite sides of a channel, and the bearing of *B* from *A* is 250°.

A ship is proceeding down channel at 16 knots on a course 195°. At 20 00 light *A* bore 135°, at 20 45 light *B* bore 240°. Construct a plotting chart to show *A*, *B* and the 20 45 fix.

How far from *B* was the ship at 20 45?

34. A 30-knot torpedo is fired at a ship steaming 12 knots at a range of 5 miles, inclination 70° left and bearing 090°.

(*a*) On what course should the torpedo be set to hit?

(*b*) In what time does it reach the target?

35. In checking a compass, the bearing of a shore object is found to be N. 30° E. If the true bearing is 019° and the variation 14° W., what is the deviation?

36. At 06 30 a ship steaming due east at 12 knots observes a light bearing Red 25°. After 20 minutes interval, the same light bears Red 50°. How far is the ship from the light at the time of the second observation and when will the light be abeam?

ANSWERS

Exercise 1

4. (a) 8·2 n.m.   (b) 4·65 n.m.   (c) 299°, 350°.

5. (a) 25 ft. 3 in.   (b) 34°.   (c) 29 ft.

6. 0·5 cm.   **7.** 062°, 027½°.   **8.** 6·5 ml.

9. (a) 030°.   (b) 2·85 n.m.   (c) 325°.   (d) 2·5 n.m.

10. 8·25 n.m.; 018° or 198°.   **11.** 118 ft.   **12.** 7·2 ml.; 5·9 ml.

Exercise 2

1. 49° 47½′ N., 5° 12′ W.   **2.** 50° 35½′ N., 4° 55½′ W.

3. 49° 52′ N., 6° 26′ W.   **4.** 50° 19′ N., 4° 41′ W.

5. 50° 03½′ N., 6° 04′ W.   **6.** Bell Buoy.

7. Manacles Bell Buoy.   **8.** Wolf Light.

9. Towan Head.   **10.** Haytor.

11. 0° 07′ S., 1° 28′ W.   **12.** 0° 29½′ N., 2° 47½′ E.

13. 0° 23½′ N., 0° 01½′ W.   **14.** 0° 06½′ N., 2° 01′ E.

15. 0° 35′ S., 0° 10′ W.

Exercise 3

1. 084°, 48 n.m.   **2.** 049°, 53 n.m.   **3.** 070°, 88 n.m.

4. 135°, 55 n.m.   **5.** 240°, 83 n.m.   **6.** 033°, 60 n.m.

7. 292°, 66 n.m.   **8.** 249°, 90 n.m.   **9.** 2998 n.m.; 198 n.m.

Exercise 4

1. 50° 34′ N., 5° 20½′ W.   **2.** 49° 53′ N., 5° 29′ W.

3. 50° 06′ N., 6° 04½′ W.   **4.** 50° 12′ N., 4° 44′ W.

5. 50° 04′ N., 5° 57½′ W.   **6.** 144° Start Pt. Lt. 9′.

7. 295° Godrevy I. Lt. 13′.   **8.** 163° Bell Buoy 15′.

9. 146° Mewstone 4′·5.   **10.** 316° Bishop Rock Lt. 15′.

Exercise 5

1. 49° 43′ N., 4° 53′ W.   **2.** 49° 55′ N., 4° 14′ W.

3. 49° 31½′ N., 5° 54′ W.   **4.** 328° Longships Lt. 8′.

5. 220° Eddystone Lt. 11′.

EXERCISE 6

1. (a) 49° 51′ N., 4° 36′ W.   (b) 090°.   (c) 13 05 hr.
2. (a) 20 00 hr.   (b) 352°.   (c) 50° 18′ N., 5° 59′ W.
3. (a) 49° 51½′ N., 5° 40′ W.   (b) 049°.   (c) 13 knots.
4. (a) 22 51½ hr.   (b) 49° 56′ N., 3° 54′ W.   (c) 23 06½ hr.
5. (a) 2 hr. 10 min.   (b) 02 05 hr.; 16′·5.

EXERCISE 7

1. N. 25° E. (Mag.).   2. S. 65° E. (Mag.).   3. S. 17° W. (Mag.).
4. S. 83° W. (Mag.).   5. N. 32° W. (Mag.).   6. N. 11° E. (Mag.).
7. S. 38° W. (Mag.).   8. S. 22° E. (Mag.).   9. N. 58° W. (Mag.).
10. N. 05° E. (Mag.).

EXERCISE 8

1. 032°.   2. 133°.   3. 207°.   4. 283°.   5. 003°.
6. 353°.   7. 156°.   8. 259°.   9. 264°.   10. 007°.

EXERCISE 9

1. 2½° W.   2. 1½° E.   3. 1° W.   4. 1½° W.   5. 1° W.
6. 2° W.   7. 1° E.   8. 1° E.   9. Nil.   10. 1° W.

EXERCISE 10

1. S. 15° W. (Mag.), 1½° E., S. 13½° W.   2. S. 49½° E. (Mag.), Nil, S. 49½° E.
3. N. 28½° W. (Mag.), ½° W., N. 28° W.   4. N. 69° E. (Mag.), 2° W., N. 71° E.
5. S. 34° E. (Mag.), ½° E., S. 34½° E.   6. S. 43° W. (Mag.), 2° E., S. 41° W.
7. N. 18½° W. (Mag.), ½° W., N. 18° W.   8. N. 04° E. (Mag.), 1° W., N. 05° E.
9. N. (Mag.), 1° W., N. 01° E.   10. S. 89° E. (Mag.), 1½° W., S. 87½° E.

EXERCISE 11

1. Nil, S. 50° E. (Mag.), 120°.   2. 1½° E., S. 21½° W. (Mag.), 213½°.
3. Nil, N. 40° W. (Mag.), 327°.   4. 2½° W., N. 47½° E. (Mag.), 039°.
5. 1° E., S. 16° E. (Mag.), 153½°.   6. 2° E., S. β2° W. (Mag.), 248½°.
7. ½° W., N. 21½° W. (Mag.), 329½°.   8. 1° W., N. 09° W. (Mag.), 002°.
9. 1½° E., S. 80½° W. (Mag.), 246°.   10. 1° W., N. 04° W. (Mag.), 352½°.

EXERCISE 12

1. 49° 47′ N., 4° 52′ W.   **2.** S. 23½° E., S. 39° W.

3. (a) 49° 46′ N., 5° 33′ W.   (b) N. 86° E.   (c) 22 15 hr.

4. 4° 52′ W., 22 10 hr.   **5.** (a) N. 58° W. (Mag.), 13′·5.   (b) 21 50 hr.

6. (a) S. 75° E.   (b) N. 77° W.   **7.** N. 43½° E., N. 03° E.

8. (a) 10′ N.   (b) 59′ E.

EXERCISE 13

1. (a) 245°.   (b) 13·2 knots.   **2.** (a) 216°.   (b) 30 n.m.

3. 49° 43′ N., 5° 21′ W.   **4.** 49° 48′ N., 4° 48′ W.

5. 49° 51′ N., 3° 54′ W.   **6.** (a) N. 62° W.   (b) 12·8 knots.

7. (a) 179°.   (b) 49° 45′ N., 4° 34′ W.

8. (a) 084°.   (b) 11·5 knots.   (c) 15 55 hr.

9. (a) 5′·5.   (b) 21 00 hr.   **10.** 2·25 knots, 090°.

EXERCISE 14

1. 087°.   **2.** 220°, 13 knots.   **3.** 299°, 9 knots.

4. 146°, 11 knots.   **5.** (a) 305°, 35 min.   (b) 145°, 24 min.

6. (a) 073°.   (b) N. 88° E.   (c) 10·6 knots.   (d) 16 40 hr.

7. (a) 265°.   (b) N. 84° W.   (c) 11·3 knots.   (d) 21 54 hr.

8. (a) 49° 45′ N., 5° 05′ W.   (b) 329°, 9 n.m.   (c) 329°, 3 knots.
    (d) S. 81° W.   (e) 12·9 knots.

9. Rame Head, 01 28 hr. **10.** (a) S. 67° W.; 16 00 hr. (b) S. 81° E.; 01 15 hr.

EXERCISE 15

1. 49° 52′ N., 5° 52′ W.   **2.** 49° 57½′ N., 6° 06′ W.

3. 50° 00′ N., 4° 49′ W.   **4.** 49° 46′ N., 5° 38′ W.

5. 50° 14′ N., 4° 10′ W.   **6.** 50° 15′ N., 4° 34′ W.

7. 50° 17′ N., 3° 25′ W.   **8.** 50° 16′ N., 4° 23′ W.

9. 50° 06′ N., 5° 48′ W.   **10.** 50° 43′ N., 4° 58′ W.

EXERCISE 16

1. 49° 47′ N., 6° 31′ W.   **2.** 49° 57′ N., 5° 56′ W.

3. 49° 55½′ N., 5° 00′ W.   **4.** 49° 58′ N., 4° 20′ W.

5. 50° 06′ N., 5° 54′ W.   **6.** 50° 02′ N., 4° 26′ W.

7. 49° 47′ N., 5° 50′ W.   **8.** 50° 06′ N., 3° 49′ W.

9. 2 knots, 222°.   **10.** 2′·5, N. 79° E.

EXERCISE 17

1. 49° 54′ N., 5° 26′ W.   **2.** 50° 01′ N., 5° 53′ W.

3. 50° 09½′ N., 6° 04′ W.   **4.** 50° 12′ N., 4° 33′ W.

5. 50° 41′ N., 5° 08′ W.   **6.** 50° 27′ N., 5° 23′ W.

EXERCISE 18

1. (a) 49° 35½′ N., 5° 47′ W.   (b) 015°.   (c) Red 80°, 130° right.

2. 186°, 14 25 hr.

3. (a) 24,000 yd., 116° right.   (b) Astern by 2′·5.   (c) 18 00 hr.

4. (a) 329°, 11 knots.   (b) 49° 47′ N., 5° 21′ W., 20 00 hr.

5. (a) 34,000 yd., Red 26°   (b) 33° right.

6. 13,500 yd., 44° left.   **7.** Ahead by 2600 yd.

8. (a) 9·4 knots right, 117 yd. per min. opening.
    (b) 9·5 knots right, 108 yd. per min. opening.

9. (a) 20,000 yd., 140 yd. per min. closing, 17·7 knots right.
    (b) 16,500 yd., 33 yd. per min. closing, 17·9 knots right.

10. Between 11 50 hr. and 12 10 hr.

NAVAL EDUCATIONAL TESTS

1. 49° 49′ N., 5° 59′ W.; 49° 52′ N., 4° 55′ W.   **2.** 265°.

3. 4360 yd.   **4.** 49° 59′ N., 4° 51′ W.; 50° 05′ N., 4° 13′ W.

5. 100° left.   **6.** 6750 ft.   **7.** 49° 55½′ N., 6° 01½′ W.

8. Red 95°, 355°, 105° right, 15,000 yd.   **9.** 263°.

10. Red 102°, 168°, 92° right, 5000 yd.   **11.** 49° 59′ N., 6° W.   **12.** 138°.

13. 50° 17½′ N., 3° 24′ W.; 49° 40′ N., 4° 44′ W.   **14.** 11 00 hr., 4800 yd.

15. 50° 15½′ N., 3° 27½′ W.; 49° 43′ N., 4° 47′ W.   **16.** 11 15 hr., 6000 yd.

17. 070°, 37 n.m.   **18.** 49° 59½′ N., 5° 56½′ W.

19. 70° right.   **20.** 268°, 24 n.m.   **21.** 50° N., 5° 55½′ W.

22. 65° left.   **23.** 9 min. 20 sec., 350 yd. ahead (approx.).

24. 084°, 3500 yd., 08 27 hr.   **25.** 020°, 3900 yd., 12 30 hr.

26. 025°, 28·5 knots.   **27.** 092°, 21·5 knots.   **28.** 136°, 12 knots.

29. 073°, 15 knots.   **30.** 295°, 2 hr. 45 min.   **31.** (a) 080°.   (b) 2° W.

32. 10 27 hr., 2 n.m., 11 12 hr.   **33.** 4 n.m.

34. 068°, 13 min.   **35.** 3° E.   **36.** 4 n.m., 07 02¾ hr.

Printed in the United States
By Bookmasters